D1708508

DESIGNED TO BECOME MORE

Designed To Become More

"The meaning of life is to find your gift
The purpose of life is to give it away"

Pablo Picasso

DONNIE L. NELSON

Dedication

I want to thank my beloved wife Denyelle, my children, Diamond and Elijah Nelson, for your ongoing support and encouragement throughout the writing of this book. You mean the world to me and I could not have done this without you. I cannot thank you enough for the sacrifices you make, allowing me the time to express and share my design with the world.

Additionally, I dedicate this book to those who are living in poverty, in a constant search for a way out. You are my inspiration. I know what it feels like to go without eating and having a survival of the fittest mentality. For me, life started from scratch, without guidance or a head start. I could be stuck, living in despair right now, but by the grace of God I made it out by discovering my gift. My heart's desire is for you to discover your gift, paving the way to a better life for you and your family.

Lastly, to the people who are searching for their why. I am also inspired by the thought of you. A thought that said, if I can help a few million people discover their gift and contribute to mankind, then more jobs will be created because people who discover who they are become empowered. They become employers that will help better the lives of countless others.

I want to be the first to say thank you for your contribution to mankind and I am eternally grateful that you are allowing me to be a part of your journey.

Table of Contents

Preface

Pablo Picasso wrote "The meaning of life is to find your gift. The purpose of life is to give it away." I wrote this book on the basis of that statement.

One day, I found myself at the worst point in life. I am talking about a point so low, I wanted to commit suicide rather than deal with the turmoil I was facing. It was at this point in my life that I began to hear the voice of the Lord clearly. I heard him say to me "You were not designed for this." Somehow, I always knew in my heart the direction I was headed in life could not be the one God designed for me. I thought there had to be more to life. This was not the path I was destined to travel.

There has to come a time in life when the void inside of you begins to speak so loudly that you can no longer ignore it. A voice that tells you that you have a WHY for being on earth, a specific reason. That you were not just born by accident but that you exist on purpose. My hope when creating this book is to help you discover who you were designed to become through helping you identify your gifts. I believe that if I can help you identify your gifts, it will lead to finding your design; your design helps you find your meaning in life so that you can begin to live life on purpose.

There is an old saying "if you search you will find". It is time that you discover who you are designed to become. Millions of people spend thousands of hours, days, months and years trying to discover the meaning of life but never will without finding their unique design (who they are to become). The meaning of life lies in who you are and not what you do. If you are anything like me, you have probably asked yourself the following questions: "Why am I here?" and "Is there something I am meant to do in life?" In my opinion, it is nearly impossible to find someone that has not asked themselves these questions. It is no coincidence that you are sitting down reading this book. To put it simply, you are not reading this book on luck or by accident or even by chance, you are reading this book on purpose. You are the only person in the world that is designed to become you. You have a purpose in life that only you can complete and the sooner you become who you were designed to be, the sooner you will find the success, happiness, and fulfillment you long for.

Today your search ends and your journey begins. It begins with discovery. Once you begin to discover your innate abilities and the gifts you were born with, you start to become self-aware. My sole purpose is to help you find your gifts so that you can discover your design. Your design is not hard to find you are not as complicated as you may think. It is time that you discover the answers to who you are designed to become. As a matter of fact, if you would like, I am offering a free personal coaching session for those of you who may have questions after reading this life-changing book. Just email me at the address found at the end of the book. The inherent abilities and gifts that God placed within you are as unique as your DNA. No one is designed to become you. God placed within you the very things that make you who you are; you just have not discovered it yet. All you have to do is be willing to experience a revelation, the one of yourself. Seek, and you will find, knock, and the door will open. You would not be reading this book if you were not searching for your design (your purpose), I am grateful you are taking steps with me to find your uniqueness. I compel you to read this book to the end and then sign up for the free coaching session. The greatest trial in life is not death, it is never obtaining a revelation of who you are to become.

Chapter 1

Becoming Who You Are Designed To Be

Life isn't about Being Yourself- It's about becoming Yourself

Wikipedia defines Vital signs as (often shortened to just vitals) a group of the 4 to 6 of the most important signs that indicate the status of the body's vital (life-sustaining) functions. These measurements are taken to help assess the general physical health of a person, give clues to possible diseases, and show progress toward recovery. Vital signs are a measurement tool that health professionals use in the preliminary diagnosis phase. The moment one of your vital signs are off balance, a flag goes up that says something is very wrong. If you are not living a life connected to your design, you start realizing that something is very wrong. You realize that your life is off balance. A flag has been thrown up.

Becoming is vital

Becoming who God designed you to be is vital to the success you see in life. Your design invents, creates and fashions the life you desire to live. It is responsible for the success or failure you see in life. Vera Wang found out how true this was on her journey to success. She began her journey as a professional figure skater but failed to make the U.S. Olympic figure-skating team at the age of 19. This helped her realize that being a professional skater was not something she was designed to become. She then turned her attention to fashion and got a job at Yves Saint Laurent boutique on New York's Madison Avenue. This led her to meet Frances Patiky Stein while shopping at Saint Laurent. Frances was one of the two fashion directors of American Vogue at the time. Frances said to the young Vera "Call me when you're finished with college." Two years later she called and got a job as a temporary assistant at American Vogue. She quickly worked her way up the ladder becoming one of the magazines youngest ever fashion editors. Like Vera Wang, when you discover what you are to become, God will bring out the potential that exists in you transforming you into what you are designed to become. So, Vera spent the next 15 years at the magazine becoming and developing her potential until she was passed over for the editor-in- chief position and decided it was time to leave to become more. She was 38 years old. She ended up taking a job at Ralph Lauren as a design director.

When you are aware of the potential that exists within you, nothing can stop you from finding out what you can become. Your potential pushes you to new boundaries. That is exactly what it did for Vera and two years later, Vera Wang became a designer with her empire being worth more than $1billion today. You will never reach true success in life without discovering what you are designed to become. Your design, who you are to become, is ultimately responsible for your achievements in life, and it is the key function to ending all of life's problems and struggles. Becoming is a part of learning who you truly are. If you are not on a constant hunt to find out who you are, you become confused, and issues with personal identity can become a challenge making success a struggle. Many things in your life will depend on your ability to find your originality, your unique design and the functions that God placed in you.

Webster defines becoming as 'to change, come, or grow to be'. Have you ever taken the time to think about what you could grow to be, or what you are capable of becoming? If you had the opportunity to change and become something different, what would it be? You were designed to become something and that something already exists in you, you just have to discover God's design for your life.

A seed placed in the wrong environment will never have the opportunity to become itself

From the time we are young, we begin to test different versions of ourselves and continue to do so at different points in life. We try to imitate the things that appeal to us the most. We do this because we do not have confidence in our own design. We have no idea who we are or what we can become. Therefore, we begin to be influenced by the people around us, not knowing that these people are struggling with their own identity and design. You will never become successful by being a cheap copy of someone else. You were not designed to become anyone else but yourself. You were not designed to become those individuals, the ones who negatively influence you. Draw your inspiration from someone who cares for you, a friend, parent, teacher, coach or celebrity. The key is to learn from those influences not to become them. The people around us exert a strong influence on our identity. That is why the choices we think we choose are ours, but in reality, those choices are probably approval seeking choices. We program ourselves to make choices that change our behavior to adapt to the approval of others. By doing this, you mold yourself into becoming something you are not. When you try to imitate others, and live up to their expectation, this becomes dangerous to your identity and design. It is difficult to try to be you and someone else at the same time. When God created you, he did not create you to be the person you idolize or look up to. He created you to be yourself because in you, are things no one else can offer.

The longer you follow the influences of others the more difficult it is to become who you were designed to be. Approximately six million searches on how to find yourself are done per month on Google. You are not the only one seeking to discover yourself and who you will become. A wide spread search in trying to discover oneself is happening across the world. Advertisements and external expectations in life create obstacles that make it difficult to become ones true self. So, figuring out how to be yourself is a necessary first step to becoming who God designed you to be.

Potential is a part of becoming

In order to begin to become the best you, you must dig to find the potential that God place inside of you. You cannot start any other place. You cannot become you without discovering your potential. Potential brings to light abilities already inside of you and helps you realize that you are more. Potential is a word that is very dear to my heart because it is the very thing that reveals your capabilities. Potential is a word that changed my life. The word potential, many people see as just a cliché, but potential is far from that. You may have heard people say "she has a lot of potential" or "he has a lot of potential." You may have heard someone say those exact words to you at least once in your life and you just think of it as just a cliché. Ultimately, you truly do not understand the meaning of the word potential. The word Potential is a key ingredient to discovering your design, so it is only right that I define potential. Potential is undiscovered ability. It is trapped power, strength you did not know you had, reserved energy, kept capacity and it is unleashed talent. Potential is everything you have the ability to become, but you have not become yet. Potential is a natural resource within you that you have not yet discovered.

Potential is energy waiting to be released. Potential is who you really are, but no one knows it yet; including you. Potential is what you can accomplish but have yet to accomplish. Potential is hidden success. The first step to becoming is believing that you have abilities in you that you have not yet seen. There is a volcano inside you waiting to erupt and come to the surface. You have things trapped inside you that want to be released. You have to understand that there is a beast inside you, lying dormant waiting to awake. Inside you is the success you have been looking for. You have a reservoir of reserve energy inside of you. It is like a car battery waiting to power up a car. Your potential is waiting to take your life to the next level. When God created you, he created you with your success already inside you. That means that whatever you were designed to become already exists within you. You already have what you are. You just have to become it.

A seed is potential

Everything God created started out as a seed and everything a seed will become exists within that seed. If a seed were placed in your hand and you were asked, "what are you holding?" What would be your answer? You would probably state "a seed." Yes, that would be true but not the whole truth. When you hold a seed in your hand, you are holding everything that seed can become. Inside of that seed is potential, and that potential was designed to become a tree, and that tree was designed to produce apples, and those apples have seeds within it to produce more trees that will produce more apples continuing its success. Every living organism that exists has its own success built in, but unless you take the necessary steps to get everything that exists within that seed; all you will ever have is a seed. A seed that has the potential to produce trees, that produce fruit, and produce more trees with more fruit. Inside you is potential and that potential leads to the discovery of your design and your design leads you to a successful life. How does a seed become what it is designed to be?

First, it has to be planted in the right environment. If you do not plant yourself in the right environment, you will never grow to be anything different. You will always look like the people you plant yourself around. You cannot hang in an environment with a bunch of people doing nothing and expect to become something. You cannot be in a pessimistic environment and expect to become optimistic about life. If you stay in an environment full of broke people, then you cannot expect to become wealthy. You will always resemble your environment. To grow, you must change your environment. A seed will never grow stuck on a tile floor. The fact you are not succeeding can be because you are planted in the wrong environment.

Second, a seed needs moisture and fertilizer. You cannot grow without being watered and fertilized. Who is watering and fertilizing you? Whoever is watering and fertilizing you is affecting your growth. They are influencing you. There are people in your life that can be toxic to your design. The people close to you can be contaminating who you will become. You must pay close attention to the people around you and take heed to what they are feeding you. If the people around you are not contributing to your design, if they are not causing you to stretch and grow than they are toxic. They are limiting your potential ultimately affecting your design. The ones who push you and make you uncomfortable, are growing you. The people who are going nowhere want you to follow, if you stay with them, your seed will dry up and die. You have to water your seed regularly. Some things to consider: What books are you reading? What lectures are you listening to? Who are you talking with? Do not let your seed become dry and die by doing nothing to grow and develop it.

Thirdly, your seed needs sunlight. You cannot grow without external influences. What classes are you taking to help you discover your potential? What seminars have you attended this year? What professional networks have you joined? You need external influences to help expose your potential. Germination is a growth process that a seed or other organism goes through. Without germination, a seed cannot become what it is designed to be. You were born with a seed hidden inside of you, but until you begin the process of self–discovery, the reality of what you are capable of becoming will never find its way to the surface. Everything that has been created was finished before its creation. A house started out as a concept in someone's mind before it is created. The clothes on your body were designed on paper before it became a reality. Just as the tree was put in the seed, what you are to become has already been put in you. You were born a finished product; you just have to discover it. God never starts anything without first finishing it. As a matter of fact, God created you so it is evident that you are finished. God told Jeremiah, "Before I conceived you in your mother's womb, I had already made you a prophet." Jeremiah's design was complete before he started his journey, just as Jesus's life was finished before he was born. Jesus did not die 2000 years ago he died long before that. The bible states "behold the lamb that was slain before the foundation of the earth was laid." Jesus was dead before he was born. He was resurrected before he was born. What you are designed to become is done, you just have to bring it to pass.

Built-in abilities

The potential of all things is hidden inside of that thing. For instance, if you were analyzing the design of an eagle and how it flies through the sky with such wonder and ease. You will discover that the eagle did not take a single day of flight school nor did it attend one class on soaring. The potential to fly already exists within the eagle itself. Flight was built into the eagle it is not something it picked up along the way. A great white shark did not take classes on how to swim or rule the ocean. It was born with the ability to swim and rule. The potential was already there.

It's already in you

That is why Potential proceeds purpose. Whatever you were designed to become, the ability to become it exists within you. God would not demand something from you that he has not put in you. David was the youngest of eight brothers and spent most of his boyhood years as a shepherd tending to his father's flock. David spent anywhere from five to ten years in this assignment. This is where he discovered that he had a heart to lead and care for others. He discovered that he possessed abilities using weaponry. He also discovered that built in him, were musical talents. Discovering who you are does not happen overnight. It takes years to develop and become you. David did not know at this point in his life that one day he would become king. David was not born into royalty, neither was his Father. He was not born with the right to be king. It is what God had designed for him to become.

Prophet Samuel

After Prophet Samuel realizes that King Saul and his descendants will not continue to rule Israel, he goes looking for another King. God led Samuel to a Town called Beit Lechem, (today its known as Bethlehem). Samuel was led by God to Bethlehem to find a man by the name of Jesse. It was among Jesse's eight sons that the next king would be found. Jesse brings forward seven of his sons, and Samuel sees that all are amazing men - physically fit, well-educated in Jewish law, and dedicated to God. They were not good enough, the Bible describes. Just as Samuel is admiring one of Jesse's other sons, he gets a message from God:

God said to Samuel, "Do not look at his countenance and at his tall stature, for I have rejected him. For it is not as man perceives it; a man sees what is visible to the eyes but God sees into the heart." (1 Samuel 16:7) KJV
So, Samuel asks: "Don't you have any more sons?" Jesse, a little flustered, responds: "Well, there still the youngest one, but he is out tending sheep."
Look where the youngest son was found; tending sheep. He was found doing what he was built to do. Your unique design will always bring you before great people.

Your gift will always bring you before great people

Jesse tells him that the youngest one is David. Samuel demands that Jesse go get him and as soon as little red-headed David appears, Samuel immediately knew he was the one. Despite the fact that he was not physically fit or impressive like his brothers. He was exactly the Leader Israel needed.

This should teach you not to judge someone by the way they look. You might have passed up the person who will be responsible for taking your life or company to the next level. The greatness of an individual is not measured by outward appearance, but by what an individual is designed to become. Samuel takes a flask of oil and pours it on David's head anointing him. When Samuel anoints David, this does not mean David becomes king. It just means he has been designated by God as next in line. Saul continues his reign not knowing what has happened, although previously, he has been told by Samuel that his days are numbered.

Show your abilities

The Bible states that the moment that David was anointed, "the spirit of God left Saul" and he fell into a dark depression. To help relieve his anger and bad moods, his advisors decide to bring in a harp player, hoping that listening to music may make the king feel better.

This is how David, still the shepherd, is brought to the palace. Again, look what led him to the presence of a King; the built-in abilities placed in him by God. David was designed with many musical abilities, including the harp. Harps were popular in the ancient world and most were much smaller than what you commonly see used today. The simplest harps were merely two pieces of wood fastened at right angles to each other with strings stretched across the wood creating a triangular shape. Strings were mostly made with twisted grass, with better strings being made of animal intestines. David plays the harp beautifully, and his playing relieves King Saul, who does not know that this youngster will soon replace him.

David and Goliath

During this period, Israel was at constant war with the Philistines. I do not know if you have ever seen the Movie Troy or the show Game Of Thrones. The movie Troy helps you form an idea of how battles were conducted in ancient times. In ancient times each side would send out its greatest champion to fight on behalf of their people. Often, the battle would end there because the losing side would become so demoralized that it would retreat. This is the same situation during this time in Jewish history. The Philistines had a champion by the name of Goliath who was a physically huge and impressive guy. To help you picture the fight that is about to take place, imagine Floyd Mayweather getting in the ring with Wladimir Klitschko. Wladimir Klitschko is 6ft '6in tall and weighed 250 plus pounds. Goliath was even bigger than him. The Jews did not have anyone in their army that compared to Goliath, as a matter of fact, they did not have a champion at all. The Jewish troops were stationed on the one side of the Elah Valley, south of Jerusalem with the Philistines on the other side. A place you can still visit today in Israel. Goliath is marching in front of the Philistine lines, shouting blasphemies at the Jews and challenging someone to come and fight him. "Choose yourself a man and let him come down to me! If he can fight me and kill me, we will be slaves to you; if I defeat him and kill him, you will be slaves to us and serve us." (1 Samuel 17:8-9) KJV

The horrified Israelite army has to listen to this because no one is willing to take on Goliath. One day, David who is still a shepherd and not a soldier shows up on the battlefield bringing food for his brothers, and he is outraged by what he sees.

The fight to become

Aggravated at Goliath's blasphemous insults of the God of Israel, David volunteers to fight Goliath. He has a hard time convincing everybody to let him go out into the field. Finally, he convinces King Saul with his steadfast faith in God:

And David said, "God who saved me from the claws of the lion and the claws of the bear, He will save me from the hands of the Philistine." (1 Samuel 17:37) KJV

To that Saul answers:

"Go and may God be with you."

David goes out to meet Goliath without sword or armor, only with his slingshot and a few stones, and his deep abiding faith in God.

Seeing him, Goliath laughs:

"Am I a dog that you come to me with sticks?"

But David is undisturbed:

"You come towards me with a sword, a spear, and a javelin, but I come to you with the name of the Lord of Hosts, the God of the battalions of Israel whom you have insulted. This day God shall deliver you into my hand, and this entire gathering shall know that it is not by a sword or with a spear that God saves..." (1 Samuel 17:47) KJV

As Goliath advances toward him, David uses his sling to launch a rock at the giant's face. It hits him in the forehead, and he falls to the ground, flat on his face. David then removes Goliath's sword and cuts off his head.

The shocked Philistines start running, pursued by the Israelite army. The end result is a marvelous victory for the Jews. Overnight David becomes a superhero. As a reward for his boldness, he is given Saul's second oldest daughter, Michal, as a wife. A song is even composed about him, and it becomes prevalent: "Saul has slain his thousands, and David his tens of thousands."

The end of Saul

The rise of David's popularity is paralleled by the rise of Saul's jealousy of him. "They have attributed to David ten thousand, while to me they have attributed thousands! He lacks only the kingship." And Saul eyed David with suspicion from that day on. It happened the next day that Saul was overcome by a spirit of envy...and he ranted incoherently in the house. David was playing the harp, and a spear was in Saul's hand. Then Saul threw the spear at David, but David alluded him twice. (I Samuel 18: 8-11)

Saul hunts him all over the country, and David has to go into hiding. But Saul has not much left to his reign; he is about to be killed in battle. The Philistines attack again—near Mount

Gilboa, in northern Israel and west of the city of Beit Shean. Saul always knew the outcome of each battle by consulting with the prophet Samuel. But now the prophet is dead. He manages to contact him in the other world, however, and Samuel tells him that he stands no chance, because God is no longer with him.

Nevertheless, Saul is no coward, and he leads the Jewish people into battle despite the odds. His sons are killed before his eyes and defeat appears inevitable. Lest he, himself, be captured by the enemy, the wounded Saul falls on his sword and dies.

The Philistines take Saul's body and remove his head, which they send on tour around the country. They hang his body and the bodies of his three sons on the walls of the city of Beit Shean, but the Jews come back at night, steal the headless body and bury it. Meanwhile, David reappears down in the south in Hebron, where he is crowned king.

Find the area you are passionate about
when it comes to serving others

For many years without any stardom, David discovered his potential (what already existed in him) while serving others. David discovered that he had leadership abilities by tending to his father's flock. He discovered that he had weaponry abilities while protecting his father's flock. David also discovered that he had musical abilities within him to soothe himself and his father's flock. On your journey to becoming you, you must find what you are most passionate about when serving others.

When you find the area you are passionate about serving others in; you discover abilities in you that you never knew existed. You will find abilities that existed from the moment of your birth. It was the discovery of these abilities that led David to national prominence. None of this would have happened for David if he had not discovered his design. When you discover the abilities you were designed with, it will lead you to a road of endless opportunities. What area(s) in life do you think you were designed for? Those areas will release your potential and help you discover what already exists in you. If you could choose right now, to follow the area you think you are designed for, what would it be?

Would it be in?

Music

Beauty

Fashion

Movies

Entertainment

Medicine

Athletics

Composition and Writing

Computer (programming and hardware)

Cooking

Baking

Mathematics

Science

Engineering

Carpentry

Woodwork

Mechanical

Outdoors

Childcare

Care for animals

Organization and planning

Management

Leadership

Teaching

Speaking

If the above list does not include an area of design that you feel you were made to operate in, take a moment to think about what you are most passionate about. It can be in one or in multiple areas. Make a mental note or write down what you selected. The potential you have inside you is located there. Are you making time to serve in those areas? Are you bringing that potential to life?

Potential never leaves you

For ten years, David was a national hero but he had to live as a fugitive for a while. He did not give into despair and he did not allow things in life to hold him back from finding his true potential. He kept perfecting his abilities by putting himself in the presence of his design. He kept practicing, he kept praying, for ten years. Then final Saul died, and He became what he was designed to be a King.

Have you avoided the area that you were designed to operate in and that you have the most potential in, on hold due to adversity, distraction, negative reactions, and experiences? Are you using your potential design despite where you are in life? No matter where you are or where you start, the area you have potential in will never leave you. The potential inside you that wants to be released will always tug at you because it is who you were designed to be. That potential will tug at you until you die or choose to release it. Those deep, passionate thoughts that you have will help lead you to your potential. That potential will help you locate your gifts, and your gifts will help you discover your purpose.

Everyone reading this book feels like there is something great inside them that they have yet to discover. What you are made to become already exists. Who you are designed to be is already done. You just have to pull it out of you.

Throughout your life, you have been given glimpses of the potential that exists in you

Glimpses of your potential were revealed to you as a child. When you were a child, you dreamed and had visions of the person you were designed to become. You pictured yourself in your adult life, you saw your future self when you were a kid. That is because your end has already been completed. Remember, everything that has been created, dead or alive was finished before its creation. Something happened along the way of you becoming you. As a kid, you had big dreams of who you were designed to become until your parents, teachers, close friends, and other people around you told you differently. You begin to become too grown-up because they helped you kill your dreams and who you were ultimately designed to become. What you saw when you were a kid or teenager was your end. When you become too grown-up, you stop thinking like a child and it is the child in you that believes things that are impossible are completely possible. A child has total confidence in their design before people come along challenging the thought of who they are and what they were designed to do. You may be broke but that is not the whole truth because on the inside of you are millions. It may be a fact right now that you are failing in life but built in you, is success beyond your imagination.

Whatever you were created to become is not on the outside of you it is inside of you.

Everything that a seed is supposed to become already exists within the seed. In you exists abilities that you did not know you had. In you exists innovation and concepts that have not yet been created. In you exists businesses that have not been thought of. In you exists books that have not been written. In you exists movies that have not been filmed. In you exists answers to the world's biggest problems. In you exists creations that the world did not know it needed. You are what you are looking for. You are what people are looking for; you just have to become it. Most of us try to copy the abilities of others when inside of you are your own abilities that the world is waiting to see. Why copy other people's abilities when you have your own that you are refusing to release? What you have always dreamed of becoming already exists, it is time to bring them to be.

Chapter 2

Designed To Function

Design is not just what it looks like and feels like.
Design is how it works." –Steve Jobs

What you are designed to become is determined by how God made you function. Therefore, your functions determine your design, your design is connected to your potential and your potential shines light on your God giving abilities. To understand what you were designed to become, you have to know what your functions are. Your functions reveal your potential and your potential exposes your true design. Your functions make-up everything you are as well as the natural abilities you possess. The functions you were born with guide your abilities to be able to fulfill your God-given purpose.

Fulfilling your function

Say for example that a person does not want to stand by the stove watching and waiting for their bread to become toasted. So, they must manufacture a machine that can bake their bread in a jiffy. Before the machine has the ability to fulfill its purpose, the manufacturer must decide how it will heat and bake the bread. This is what we call a function. The function determines an activity or how an object or person operates. After the manufacturer decides how to heat and bake bread, (s)he must design that as an ability into the machine. Essentially, the function becomes the determining factor in how something is designed. Thus, the function and design of the machine are inseparable. For further clarification, Webster defines Function as an action performed by a device, department, or person that produces a result. When you were created, you were designed in a way that would allow you to fulfill your function. That is why you have certain qualities and characteristics. You were designed to be able to complete the purpose you were intended for. The abilities you have to function are inherent, they existed within you before your birth.

Let's go a little deeper by looking at how a toaster functions. As previously stated, before the machine has the ability to fulfill its purpose, the manufacturer must decide how it will heat and bake the bread. The heating mechanism becomes a function of the machine. Electrical energy flows into a toaster from an outlet in the house connected with wire. The electric current flows through a series of thin filaments connected together but spaced widely enough apart to toast the whole bread surface. The filaments are so thin that they glow red when the electricity flows through them. Like a series of small radiators, the filaments beam heat toward the bread in the toaster. The steady supply of heat rapidly toasts the bread. There are filaments on each wall of the toaster, so the two sides of the bread are toasted simultaneously. These are the functions needed for the machine to fulfill its purpose. Without these functions, the toaster would not be able to carry out its reason for existing. God created and designed you in a way that would allow you to fulfill your functions. Your outgoing personality, gift of gab, ability to sing, creative mind, ability to produce magic with your hands, effortlessness communication skills, will to bring ideas and thoughts to life, your nature to lead or to follow to inspire, to analyze and to see the bigger picture, and your natural problem-solving abilities all are a part of your functions and personality.

Performing your function

Whatever God designed you to become, you have the ability to be. Functions that were built in you before you were born give you the ability to perform your purpose.

If you can perform like a teacher, never being taught how to effectively teach, then you have a natural function and design that helps you fulfill that role.

If you can perform like a singer, never being taught to hold a single note, then you have a natural function to sing and a design that helps you fulfill that role.

If you can perform like an engineer, never being taught how to make processes run efficiently, then you have a natural function and a design that helps you fulfill that role.

If you can perform like a dancer, never being taught how to dance, then you have a natural function and design that helps you fulfill that role.

If you can perform like a chef, never being taught how to cook. Then you have a natural function to cook and a design that helps you fulfill that role.

If you can perform like a servant, never being taught how to serve, then you have a natural function to serve and a design that helps you fulfill that role.

If you can perform like a leader, never being taught how to lead then you have a natural function to lead and a design that helps you fulfill that role.

If you can perform like a public speaker, never being taught how to speak publically, then you have a natural function to speak and a design that helps you fulfill that role.

If you can perform like an artist, never being taught how to create art, then you have a natural function to create art and a design that helps you fulfill that role.

If you can perform like a fashionista, never working one day in the fashion industry, then you have a natural function for fashion and a design that helps you fulfill that role.

If you can perform like a beauty guru, never taking a single class on beauty. Then you have a natural function to create beauty and a design that helps you fulfill that role.

If you can perform like a counselor, with no background in counseling, then you have a natural function to counsel and a design that helps you fulfill that role.

If you can perform in a specific athletic position, without ever being taught that position, then you have a natural function for athletics and a design that helps you fulfill that role.

If you can perform as an actor, without ever being taught how to act. Then you have a natural function to act and a design that helps you to fulfill that role.

No one taught a bird how to fly; how to soar the skies and function in the air. It was already built into the bird because that is its natural function. Its wings, the weight of its body, and everything else that makes a bird a bird was all designed in a way that allows the bird to fly. No one taught a fish how to function in water; how to swim was already built into the fish. Its fins, and the unique shape of its body were all designed to help the fish carry out its natural function to SWIM.

I have never taken a single public speaking class but when I speak, people may assume I have a degree in public speaking. That function was already built in me before I was born. I was designed for it. I have all the necessary functions I need to operate as a speaker. No one has to teach you what you already do naturally. Your functions are a part of your nature they make up who you are. Your functions give you the ability to operate uniquely in the area you are gifted in. No one taught Bill Gates how to make better software than IBM he was already designed that way. Your natural abilities allow you to function the way that you do and no one has to teach them to you. Pause for just a second and ask yourself this question. What are my natural functions? Write it down on a piece of paper or in your smartphone. Do not move from this sentence until you can list at least one natural function that you think you may possess.

Not everyone can function like you

I have noticed over the years that when people operate in their function, they may not see it as a gift because it is something they naturally do. They never look at their function as something great or amazing. They look at it as if it is something that everyone can do, but everyone cannot do what you are capable of doing. What you see as easy others may see as hard. It is easy to you because you were born with that particular function, but people who do not have your function are challenged by the task. Not everyone has the ability to do mathematics, to sing, to act, to speak, to engineer, to teach, to write code, to dance, to create beauty, to invent, to create fashion, to lead, etc. Every function that you have is designed to help you fulfill your why.

Function in your natural environment

Your function determines your environment. A bird is happiest not when it's in a cage or birdhouse, eating food or on the ground where it baths, but in the air where it is allowed to use its function. The fish is happiest when it is in water, why, because the water allows the fish to use its function. There is an environment waiting for you that you naturally belong in. God will place you in environments that you may think are wrong for you, but those environments are meant to shape you into what you are to become. If you could quit your job right now and be in an ideal environment that would allow you to use your function, where would you go to put your functions to use?

Would you go to a classroom?

Would you go to a stage?

Would you go behind a camera?

Would you go on the field?

Would you go into the kitchen?

Would you go into a hospital?

Would you go into a church?

Would you go into the lab?

Would you go capture the wonders of the world?

Would you go into the fashion world?

Would you go into the beauty industry?

Would you go help the sick?

Would you go help the homeless?

Would you go help rescue kids?

Would you go help animals?

Would you go help broken men?

Would you go help battered women?

Would you go to a recording studio?

You feel your happiest and most fulfilled when you are in an environment that causes you to use your functions. Are you in an environment that causes you to use your functions? If you find an environment that allows you to be yourself, you have found an environment that allows you to use your functions and to operate in your design.

Design is inherent

To remove your function would significantly change who you are because your functions inform and reveal your nature and your design. Your design is inherent and necessary for you to fulfill your purpose. Your design represents the complete make-up of who you are. As stated in this chapter previously, your functions determine your design. So, if you were designed to sing then your voice, your lungs, your vocal cords, the ability to recall tunes and tonal sequences, the rhythm of your heartbeat, and the way you perceive melodies are all designed to create the music you have in you.

If you were designed to be a photographer, to capture the wonders of life, you will have an eye for beauty and aesthetics. You have the intellectual capacity to perceive beauty and communicate it to others in photos or words of expression. If you are designed to teach then you were born with the intellectual capacity to retain an enormous amount of information with the ability to sort and structure it in a way that you can transfer the information to others. You were also born with excellent communication skills, patience, ideal productivity and an inclination to work with others. You were born to make people think. You were born to inspire and motivate. You were born to learn fast. The very essence of who you are designed to become accommodates your functions.

Are not two sparrows sold for a penny? Yet not one of them will fall to the ground outside your Father's care. 30 And even the very hairs of your head are all numbered. 31So don't be afraid; you are worth more than many sparrows. Matthew 10:29-31 NIV.

The very hairs on your head were manufactured by God. Everything you are and will be is designed by your Father in heaven. The way you look, the color of your skin, your height, the language you speak, your physical attributes, and your intellectual capacity are all a part of how God designed you; attributes to help you fulfill your purpose. Your design will always relate to your purpose. It is a natural, innate, intimate part of who you are. Your functions will predict your nature, and your nature is that which you inherently are. Your nature expresses the very purpose of your existence.

Function will always predict the nature of a thing

I define ability as possessing the power or capacity of being able or fit to do something. Webster defines natural as

53

existing in or formed by nature. When you were born, built in you were specific functions, and those functions gave you the power and ability to do things that others around you cannot do.

Before I formed you in the womb, I knew[a] you, before you were born I set you apart; I appointed you as a prophet to the nations."
Jeremiah 1:5 NIV

The very thing Jeremiah was designed to become, God built in him before he was born. Jeremiah was born with the natural ability to be a prophet. If you study the life of Jeremiah, you will find that the essence of his make-up, of his design, are his abilities to be a prophet. Everyone is born with a unique set of functions and those functions are identified by your natural abilities. They make you who you are. They may be artistic, intellectual, physical, organizational and so on. They are inherently a part of you. Your natural ability is such a part of what you are, that they are sometimes latent, unrecognized and unused until certain circumstance in life cause them to come forward. This causes us to discover an innate ability we knew nothing about. You have so much built in your nature that is undiscovered that you must find. How often have you sat down and thought about your Aptitudes? Aptitudes are natural abilities or inclinations for certain types of functions.

Aptitudes

For example, if a child can draw a picture in his mind and bring it out in an art form, then his spatial aptitude is high. He may not already be an artist or Leonardo De Vinci, but the function or Aptitude is there. Spatial Aptitude indicates a person's ability to visualize things in space.

What are your aptitudes, your natural born abilities? Here are a few examples of aptitudes.

Were you born with Verbal or non-verbal communications abilities? – Can you write or speak in a way that transfers ideas, emotions, or information. Can you give a lecture, act out your feelings, or write poetry? These are all methods of communication aptitude. If you can, then you have a **verbal and non-verbal communication aptitude, natural born verbal and non-verbal communication abilities.**

Were you born with verbal comprehension abilities? - Can you demonstrate an empathetic understanding of ideals or emotions in verbal or nonverbal communication? Can you express sympathy for a friend's problem? Do you know all the current gossip, and do you have the ability to persuade people to do things? **Then you have Verbal comprehension aptitude, natural born verbal comprehensive abilities.**

Were you born with Logical abilities? – Can you apply thought or logic to problems? Do you have the ability to see the resolution before having a solution to the problem? Do you know exactly what to do in a given situation? Are you able to calculate in your mind weather something will work or not? **Then you have a Logical aptitude, natural born logical abilities.**

Were you born with Artistic abilities? – Are you visually creative, do you have musical abilities or dramatic talents. Can you draw, take amazing photographs, dance, or design an outfit and apply makeup very well? **Then you have an Artistic aptitude natural born artistic abilities.**

Were you born with Mechanical abilities? – Can you recognize the connection between parts of machines, the way things are made, and finding ways to make things work more efficiently? Can you hook up a car stereo in an automobile? Can you take apart something and put it back together? Can you build a house? **Then you have a Mechanical aptitude, natural born mechanical abilities.**

Were you born with Numerical abilities? – Do you love to work with numbers? Do you like solving math problems?

Do you like knowing how many miles your car gets per gallon and budgeting your finances or the finances of others? **Then you have a Numerical aptitude, natural born numerical abilities.**

Were you born with Clerical abilities – Are you always arranging and recording numbers and letter combinations. Are you always alphabetizing or putting items in a specific order, filing reports, typing information, and keeping records? **Then you have a Clerical aptitude a natural clerical ability.**

Were you born with Spatial abilities – Do you have an understanding of how parts of things fit together or a multidimensional understanding? Are you able to put together a jigsaw puzzle, rearrange furniture attractively in a room, or putting together model cars? **Then you have a Spatial aptitude a natural born spatial ability.**

Were you born with Physical abilities? – Do you have bodily strength and coordination, and manual dexterity? Do you love playing sports, lifting weights, moving furniture, and building things? **Then you have a Physical aptitude natural born physical abilities.**

Were you born with Organizational abilities? – Do you like implementing and evaluating actions for yourself or others? Do you like planning parties, promoting parties, planning a vacation, marketing or conducting events? **Then you have an Organizational aptitude, a natural born organizational ability.**

Were you born with Intellectual abilities? - Are you a creative thinker, fast learner, forward thinker, or a developer of concepts? Do you like teaching, studying, reading, finding new ways to do things, and developing plans to increase the value of something? **Then you have an Intellectual aptitude, natural born Intellectual abilities.**

These are just some of the aptitudes that I have named, but there are many more. You have to discover the functions that are built in you. As stated previously "if you seek you will find."

I once read a book by Ken Robinson called "Finding Your Element." I definitely recommend reading this book on your search to discovering yourself. In his book Finding your Element, Ken spoke about four tests that I think would be beneficial in discovering your unique design. The first test he suggested is the GATB know as the General Aptitude Test Battery. The assessment was created by the U.S Department of Labor to measure nine different aptitudes that assess the success you can expect in a specific career or business. It helps you measure what you are naturally designed to do.

The GATB measures general learning ability, verbal aptitude, spatial aptitude, form perception, clerical perception, motor co-ordination, finger dexterity, manual dexterity.

The GATB can only be administered by someone who has completed GATB certification. The test consists of 12 parts that you will be asked only most of the time to complete some of the GATB, but not all.

The second test he suggests taking was The Gallup Strength Finder test. It is an online assessment that helps you identify your potential and strengths. It was created by Dr. Donald O. Clifton and a team of scientists at Gallup. The assessment consists of 177 questions that cover a wide range of aptitudes.

The third test he suggests taking is the Career Scoop test administered by The Vocational Research Institute. The Career Scope test assesses your interests and aptitudes, combines those to give you recommendations. Recommendations about careers you may enjoy and be successful doing, and what courses or training programs you should focus on in order to pursue those careers or businesses.

The last test he suggested was the O*Net ability profiler. It is an assessment created by Occupational Information Network. It helps you identify occupations that fit your natural abilities. This assessment also tests you in the same nine areas as the GATB.

These aptitudes or born abilities we possess will manifest more as we develop and mature, as chances for their use or expression arise, and as our environment brings about their development. You must never allow anyone or any environment to repress and trap your abilities. The moment you allow this to happen, you stop becoming yourself. The functions, natural abilities, and innate abilities that you were born with are all a part of your work.

Chapter 3

Designed To Fulfill Your Work

Doing what you were designed to do is you working

Webster defines work as an activity involving mental or physical effort done in order to achieve a purpose or result. Your work is what you were born to achieve. There is no educational system or class that can teach you how to become something you were designed to be. There is no system that can teach you how to achieve your life's purpose, or at least, one has not yet been created. The more aware you become of your functions, the more you began to discover your work, and your work will lead you to discover your life's true design.

Work willingly at whatever you do, as though you were
working for the Lord rather than for people. 24 Remember
that the Lord will give you an inheritance as your reward,
and that the Master you are serving is Christ.[e]
Colossians 3:23-24 NLT

Throughout life we have been taught that work is

something we do, not something we are designed to become.

Your work is what you will become. God wants you to work

to become all that he designed you to be. When you work

like you are working for God instead of people, you become

yourself. You are not pressured to be something you are not

in order to be accepted by people who do not even know who

they are. Once you find what it is that you are designed to

do, you never stop working. Have you ever heard someone

say that if you do what you love, then you will never work

another day in your life? This statement, in itself, embodies

being yourself and following your own unique design. When

you are doing what you love, you are being yourself. When

your work allows you to be yourself, it will never feel like

work. Have you ever heard anyone say that they love doing

something they hate, no? People are not fulfilled in their jobs because they are continuously becoming something they were never designed to be.

When you believe that work is something you do versus something you are then you will continue doing things that you dislike. You cannot continue to look for a job that has nothing to do with your design. It just becomes a waste of time when you are trying to become something you were never meant to be. You cannot allow a job to trap your work. So many people allow this to happen and that is why they are depressed; every Monday going to a job that does not help them fulfill their design. Are you trapped in a job that does not allow you to become who you were designed to be?

Do you continue to go to a place that is not you?

I do not want you to think that I am saying jobs are a bad thing, in fact, the last job I had prepared me for my work

65

because it allowed me to operate in my design. It allowed me to develop my speaking and teaching gift. So, every now and then, your work will create your job. I found this to be true with my wife. She worked as the General Manager of a shoe and clothing store. This job allowed her to express her gift for fashion and style. This led her to start a fashion blog which has become very successful. One reason for her success is the connection she found in her design. She tells me all the time that it never feels like work even though she works all day. Your future is in your work. Think beyond your job.

One day as Jesus was standing by the Lake of Gennesaret,[a] the people were crowding around him and listening to the word of
God. 2 He saw at the water's edge two boats, left there by the fishermen, who were washing their nets. 3 He got into one of the boats, the one belonging to Simon, and asked him to put out a little from shore. Then he sat down and taught the people from the boat.

4When he had finished speaking, he said to Simon, "Put out into deep water, and let down the nets for a catch."
5Simon answered, "Master, we've worked hard all night and haven't caught anything. But because you say so, I will let down the nets."

6When they had done so, they caught such a large number of fish that their nets began to break. 7 So they signaled their partners in the other boat to come and help them, and they came and filled both boats so full that they began to sink. 8 When Simon Peter saw this, he fell at Jesus' knees and said, "Go away from me, Lord; I am a sinful man!" 9 For he and all his companions were astonished at the catch of fish they had taken, 10 and so were James and John, the sons of Zebedee, Simon's partners.

Then Jesus said to Simon, "Don't be afraid; from now on you will fish for people." 11 So they pulled their boats up on shore, left everything and followed him. –Luke 5:1-11 NIV

Before Peter found his true work, God was using his Job to develop him into what he was to become, a fisherman.

Ask yourself this question, is your current job helping develop your functions? Is it helping you develop your work and who you are to become? Your job is designed to help develop your gift, to help develop your functions, to help develop who you are to become, not to develop who you are not to become. Do not waste your time in a place that does not help you become what you are designed to be.

Your gift can never be fired

You must understand that your work is not your job. Your work is what you were designed to do. What you are born to become is your work. Your job is simply what they pay you to do, your job is your skill. Your work is your natural function, something you were designed for. A skill is something you learn, but natural ability is inherent, it is not something learned. You can be replaced by someone else with the same learned skill at a job. In other words, you can always be fired from a job, but you can never be fired or laid you off from being yourself. When you leave a job, you take your work: your innate abilities, functions, and design, with you. Steve Jobs was fired by the very company he co-founded, but he was not fired from his work, his own unique design.

In his renowned speech to the Stanford graduating class of 2005, Jobs admitted he "really didn't know what to do for a few months." He added,

"I felt that I had let the previous generation of entrepreneurs down, that I had dropped the baton as it was being passed to me. I even thought about running away from (Silicon) Valley. But something slowly began to dawn on me. I still loved what I did. The turn of events at Apple had not changed that one bit. And so, I decided to start over." And he did just that.

He went right back to operating in his unique design and co- founded a new computer company called NeXT and also launched Pixar Animation Studios. His work, his unique designed followed him. As both companies began to see success, they become acquired by other companies. NeXT was purchased by Apple and Pixar was purchased by Disney. Apple knew that acquiring NeXT would help return Steve Jobs to the already struggling company at the time. One year after the purchase of NeXT Steve Jobs became Apple's CEO taking the struggling company back to success creating the iPod, iPhone, and iPad. Your work will be found in your design. When you do what you are designed for, nothing can stop your success.

Jobs put it this way in the remaining part of his speech

"I didn't see it then, but it turned out that getting fired from Apple was the best thing that could have ever happened to me. The heaviness of being successful was replaced by the lightness of being a beginner again, less sure about everything. It freed me to enter into one of the most creative periods of my life," he said. "I'm pretty sure none of this would have happened if I hadn't been fired from Apple. It was awful tasting medicine, but I guess the patient needed it. Sometimes life hits you in the head with a brick. Don't lose faith. I'm convinced the only thing that kept me going was that I loved what I did. You've got to find what you love."

Wherever you go, you can plant your natural abilities, so it can start to prosper you again. You are much more than your job, than the place that you work. Nobody can fire you from that. Having a job is a great thing but finding your true work is everything. As you can see in the example given about Steve Jobs, this book is designed to shift your thinking so that you can find yourself. When you find yourself, you will gain a new perspective regarding what you were created to do on this earth, instead of just being reactive to your environment.

You were not created just to punch a clock, you were created to fulfill a purpose. You were created to contribute to your generation. The functions you were born with are built into you, so that you can make a difference in the world. The world needs you. The people you see every day need you and you need them as well. You may not know what is in you just yet, but this book is destined to bring it out. The innate abilities and your functions were given to you to fulfill your purpose, your why. Fulfilling your purpose can happen wherever you go. Work is ongoing throughout your life on this earth. Your job is only your career for a small portion of your life; it is temporary. You can lose your job tomorrow. Your whole career can end today, but your work is something that you will have to complete until the very day you die, you can never lose that. It will not matter how many times you move around; you will still have what you were born with. It does not matter if you have been abused, neglected or mistreated you still carry what you were born with on the inside of you. Your design cannot be worn out; it cannot be dismissed nor taken away because it's you. For your work to leave you, would in essence mean that you no longer exist. You were designed in a specific way for a specific reason. When you discover your work, and how you were born to function, you will find that reason. Your job is not your work, so pay close attention to the differences, this will allow you to start discovering your real work, your true functions, whether or not it happens in your job environment or not.

Let me explain what I mean. Picture yourself having a job as a coach and that you are very successful. Imagine people telling you daily that you are an amazing coach. Does that mean coaching is an innate ability of yours and your true work? Not precisely, but having the ability to inspire and help people discover their potential is. You are designed in a way that enables you to inspire and help people discover their potential, this supports your job choice of being a coach. Your work is your ability to help people become more whether it be through writing a book, speaking or inspiring.

Let me give you another example. Let's say you are a physician. Does that mean that being a doctor is something you are designed to be? No, but it is your job, although in your position, you may find your gifts of benevolence, empathy, compassion, and serving. Let's say you never became a doctor, but rather you spent all of your life volunteering to help those in need. You could have expressed that same innate ability and that same inherent design. Your work is benevolence, empathy, and a compassion for serving others.

Your job is temporary, but your work is permanent.

Your job is your skill, but your gift is your work. You can be fired from your job, but you can never be fired from what you are designed to be. As stated by Myles Munroe in his book Pursuit of Purpose "Your life purpose may seem to be in seed form right now, you will realize that your work is your seed. Your work is your seed, and your seed is your work."

"As you plant your gift, you grow in your work; you multiply it. A tiny seed carries within it the capacity to become a mighty fruit-bearing tree."

You are defined by your work

You are defined by your work, and your work is directly related to your function. That is why your functions reveal who you are. An apple seed is revealed by its ability to become a tree. A bird is revealed by its ability to fly. That is why when a bird is flying it is working and operating in its design. When a seed starts to become a tree, it is working; it is fulfilling its design. Just as a bird is defined by flying and a fish is defined by swimming, so are you defined by your work (by your design).

For example, when you think of LeBron James, you think basketball player. When he is on the court, he is working, he is doing what he was designed to do. When you think of Steve Jobs, you think of Apple or creator of the iPhone. When he was in the office designing iPhones, creating software and computers, he was working, doing what he was designed to do.

When you think of TD Jakes or Joel Osteen, you think of a preacher, pastor, and a great speaker. When they are standing at the podium speaking the Word of God, they are working, doing what they were designed to do. When you think of Beyoncé, you think of music. When she is creating music, recording in the studio, or on stage performing, she is working, doing what she was designed to do. When you think of Stephen King, you think of movies and books. When he is creating movies and books, he is working, doing what he was designed to do. All of the above people are defined by their work.

The moment I stated those names, you immediately identified them by their work, by what they were designed to become. When people think of you, what do they think about? How do they identify you? When I'm teaching people how to identify their gifts and when I am on stage giving a lecture to help people discover who they are, I am working. Writing this book is me fulfilling my work, it is me doing what I am designed to do. It is your work that makes you valuable. When a person finds his work, what he was designed to do, everything around him comes alive.

Chapter 4

Discovering Your Function

If you get the inside right, the outside will fall into place.
Primary reality is within; secondary reality without."
— Eckhart Toll

When you were born, inherently in you were specific functions. Those functions can be athletic, mathematical, intellectual, artistic, or creative. You may have the functions to sing, act dance, public speak, teach, talk, entertain, engineer, and/or innovate. Whatever it may be, everyone inherently has a function that gives them the ability to do something. Do you remember when you learned how to walk? The answer is probably no because it's a disposition. That ability was placed in you before you were born. Your functions are the same way; they were built in you before you were born. They become such a part of you that you don't recognize them. What are your function/s? Do me a favor, participate in a few exercises with me in this chapter. Participating in these exercises will help you locate your natural functions and/or gifts.

Exercise 1

Grab a pen and paper or just pull out your smartphone and write down some things you are able to do effortlessly.

The function/s you were born with have equipped you with abilities that allow you to do certain things you find really easy. These are things that take little to no effort on your part but might give others a hard time. Do you catch yourself helping people with a particular task? It is likely because you are great at it, whether you realize it or not. If you think about it, people have likely been telling you that you are great at something for a long time. You just were not listening. You might think your functions are only something you are great at doing because it is a part of your nature, but sometimes our functions are the things we do not even think about. If people describe you as a creative thinker, and you are confident in those abilities to come up with new ideas, your functions will be innovative. You should consider becoming an entrepreneur or a marketing genius. People describe my wife as a fashionista because she is confident in her visual abilities. She can see the finished product before people can even form the idea in their minds of what something will look like. This function provides her the ability to create new trends, and it also gives her an eye for anticipating what her audience will respond to next. This function gives her the ability to become a fashion designer or fashion stylist. How do people describe you when you are not around? Do they describe you as being loud, funny, creative, athletic, computer savvy, talkative, intellectual, a dancer, or good with your hands? However, people describe you will correlate to the functions that are inherent in you.

Joseph was descried as a dreamer and that very function leads him to become the second person in command in Egypt in his time.

19 "Here comes that dreamer!" they said to each other. 20 "Comenow, let's kill him and throw him into one of these cisterns and say that a ferocious animal devoured him. Then we'll see what comes of his dreams." – Genesis 37:19 NIV

The functions you possess are simply something you do better than most. Are there things that you find really easy or obvious to do, while others may struggle or juggle their way through it? I know I find speaking super easy and I believe that others should find it to be just as easy, but that is not how it works in life. Instead, I find that others struggle while I stand there feeling like it is a cake walk. If there is anything that comes naturally to you that does not seem so natural to others, it is called a function. That is why it is critical to take a long hard look at what you do effortlessly.

Maybe you are great at explaining things or giving good advice. Maybe you are great at making people laugh or entertaining them using no effort at all. Maybe you are great at organizing or planning, or maybe you are great at drawing graphs or working with numbers. Maybe you are great at singing, or acting, maybe you are great at styling or designing, or maybe you are great at observing things or having an eye for beauty. Maybe you are great at reporting things or telling stories, or maybe you are great at writing or thinking of new things. Whatever it maybe you are great at something. You may have never paid attention to what you are actually great at. This brings us to exercise number 2.

Exercise 2

There are family, friends, and associates around you that observe you in a way that you cannot observe yourself.

Ask everyone you know that will give you an honest assessment of what they think you are naturally great at. Their insight will be valuable, informative, enlightening, endorsing and reinforcing. Their observations have greater insight than a self-analysis. Ask a lot of people that know you but be sure to always ask them one-on-one. Ask these four questions.

1. What makes me unique?

2. What do you think I do particularly well using no effort?

3. What is my strongest skill or characteristic?

4. What do you think I'm naturally good at?

Compile the results and you will discover the function you were unaware you had.

Everything those individuals expressed to you, are all things that come naturally to you, and they have always been in you since the day you were born. You may have never thought of them as a function, but those functions you have, everyone else does not. Your functions can also be discovered in other ways. Your functions can be discovered through television shows you love and cannot get enough of. It can be discovered through books and magazines that you read regularly and are based on a particular topic. A topic that entices you to dig further and further as your desire to learn more increases. Think about what it is that you love to do most when you have free time. If you are drawn toward it, it is a natural function. What you are and who you are come out of you when things like television shows and books elicit those functions you were born with. For example, those who are role models to you, spark things in you because it helps you identify traits in you that they possess. Those abilities that you know you have and that you share with them cause you to try living through them as you watch them perform their functions. You do not have to live through them, you have a similar function. The only difference between you and them is that they are aware of their functions and they put it out there for the world to see. The exercise that we are about to go over, you have probably heard before. That is because it is, not just something merely stated, it is something that has been found to be factual on many occasions in the life of successful people.

Exercise 3

Think back as far as you possibly can when you were a child. Think back to times when you were not influenced by your environment, your friends, teachers, peers or fears. Back to the times when your parents' expectations of you were to be outside playing and exploring in a safe and secure environment. They were simple expectations.

What did you do?

How did you fill your days?

What were your favorite things to play?

What did you do that everyone else wished they could do?

What did you find fun to do in your alone time? What did you dream of becoming?

These questions express your inborn abilities. They help you see what functions were operating in you as a child. If your favorite thing as a child was to put together puzzles, then you probably function as a natural problem solver. That is why people come to you with their problems all the time. As I kid, I loved to play games where I was the leader or teacher. Thinking back to those days, I recognize that the functions I had to lead and teach were always in me. It has always been a part of who I am. To this very day, I love leading people to discovering who they are and schooling them on how they can become more. Your functions have always been there, you just were unaware of them.

Everyone loves to operate in their functions. I have noticed that when people are operating in their function, they have no sense of time. Time becomes lost when you are doing things that are connected to who you are. When you find activities that are a part of your functions you become so engrossed in them that you do not think about time, eating or sleeping, and you actually have to remind yourself to eat and sleep.

Exercise 4

In this exercise, you must identify where you lose your sense of time by answering these questions on a piece of paper or on your smartphone.

Where do you get lost in time?

This will always point toward areas that are part of your natural functions and deep passions. If you only focus on what people are willing to pay you for and what you can become the best at, then you will not be able to discover your passion. The passion that you will need to push you out of your comfort zone to achieve something great. This would be like Steve Jobs choosing to work at Best Buy as General Manager rather than embracing his natural function for computer innovation and hardware design. He probably would have been perfectly happy, but he would not have revolutionized the computer and smartphone industry. Just like Steve Jobs, we must find our natural function if we want to make a difference in the lives of ourselves and others.

Chapter 5

Refining Your Seed

"Society has little to do with how refined a man's gift is; it rather depends on his will to learn."

Everything was born with a seed inside of it; from animals to fruit, to plants, and to humans. The purpose of this chapter is to make you aware of what type of seeds you have inside of you. In the previous chapter, we spoke about functions and how they give you the ability to perform in your own unique way. Well, those functions we talked about were born out of a specific seed. Inside of every seed is a tree/plant, and that tree/plant has a unique function, and that function is called a gift. For example, if you were born with a singing seed than you have a singing function and that function provides you the ability to produce a wonderful sound with your voice. If you fully participated in the exercises in the previous chapter, then you should be somewhat aware of the seed/s that you possess inside of you because those seeds help you function the way you do today.

Do you have a creative seed?

Do you have an engineering seed? Do you have an artistic seed?

Do you have a numbers seed?

Do you have a problem- solving seed? Do you have writing seed?

Do you have an acting seed?

Do you have a cooking and baking seed? Do you have a carpentry seed?

Do you have a Mechanical seed? Do you have a childcare seed?

Do you have an organizing or planning seed? Do you have a fashion or design seed?

Do you have an entrepreneurial or innovator seed? Do you have a leadership seed?

Do you have a teaching or speaking seed?

Do you have a marketing and advertising seed?

You possess within you some type of seed and that seed has within it, a gift. Inside every apple seed is an apple tree, and that tree produces a fruit called an apple which is the seed's gift. I have a speaking and teaching seed that produced an ability to communicate in a compelling way. Therefore, I'm gifted at speaking and lecturing. Discovering the gift born out of your seed is a vital part of understating who you are and what you are capable of becoming. Discovering the seed that carries your gift helps you locate your purpose and your destination in life. Lastly, discovering the seed that carries your gift helps you find your value in life, and your value translates into worth, and worth creates wealth.

While the earth remains, seedtime and harvest, cold and heat, summer and winter, and day and night shall not cease. Gen 8:22 NKJV

What God is revealing within this verse is that there are established, inherent laws within creation. Laws are established principles, meaning they will work the same way every single time for anyone who gets involved with them. For instance, gravity is a natural law, it works the same way for everyone. If the Law of Gravity did not exist than anything you throw into the air would just float. Since the Law of Gravity is a real thing, then what you throw in the air or off a building will be pulled down by gravity. This law will work the same way, every single time no matter how big or small something is. There are spiritual and physical laws. They represent established natural patterns within creation. Once you learn the laws of something, you learn the success or failure that law produces. If you learn the laws of your workplace, your business, or your relationships you will find that they produce success if you follow them. You also will find that they produce failure when you do not follow them. Everything God has designed operates within the Seed Law to bring an increase into the life of every living thing, from humans to plants, to animals. Yes! The kingdom of God works on the seed principle. Everything you were created to be is a finished product in the form of a seed. You have all the characteristics and capabilities you will ever need to become who God designed you to be. In fact, everything that God created started out as a seed and we see this in Gen 1:11-12 NIV

Then God said, "Let the land produce vegetation: seed-bearing plants and trees on the land that bear fruit with seed in it, according to their various kinds." And it was so. 12 The land produced vegetation: plants bearing seed according to their kinds and trees bearing fruit with seed in it according to their kinds. And God saw that it was good."

Every human, plant, and animal that God created was given the ability to multiply and replenish. You were constructed for continuous increase. That increase is wrapped in a seed form that must be planted and taken through the established principles to grow and develop to fully produce its increase. Then and only then will you get the power out of the seed that it carries. So, what are the principles? I'm glad you asked, let me begin by fully explaining the principles of a seed. If you were to place a seed in the corner of your living room or kitchen floor, it would remain there forever as a seed. You will never get to experience the fruit of that seed because that seed is planted in the wrong environment.

The Law of every Seed

Principle 1

A seed must be placed in the right environment for it to begin its process of becoming what it was designed to be. You have to choose your association and education.

A seed will only begin to grow in soil, it cannot produce on concrete or tile floor, just in soil. If you are in the wrong environment, your seed will not be able to release its fruit. That is why it is critical for you to choose your association. Have you ever heard the saying "birds of a feather flock together"? Eagles do not hang with pigeons, owls do not hang with hawks. Eagles associate with other eagles because they help develop one another. A pigeon cannot develop an eagle. If you are a dancer and all you associate with are computer engineers, you will never grow to become the dancer you were designed to be. You must associate yourself with individuals that can develop your seed not hinder it. It is the same way with education. If you know you are a computer engineer, why would you study journalism? It is important to know your seed so you can pick the right education. The environment that you place yourself in will either grow your seed or trap your seed. It is my guess that if you are reading this book, then you would like to grow your seed. Place yourself in an environment that can develop your seed. You must find your soil. If your gift is in teaching, then find an environment that is capable of producing teachers and plant yourself in that soil.

Principle 2

For a seed to become a tree, it must isolate itself.

A seed must take itself away from the earth and hide in the ground. How often are you hiding yourself to refine you seed? How often do you go away from everyone to seek and find who you really are? How often do you isolate yourself to read the necessary books on your gift and listen to the essential lectures to develop your gift? You have to learn to get away to spend time with yourself. You have to get to know you better, and the only way to do that is giving yourself some space. If you pack your life with so many tasks and activities on a daily basis, you will have no time to breath, let alone get to know yourself. You cannot become a victim of a schedule that will not allow you to develop who you are. You need space so that you can focus, inspire, and excite yourself about discovering your seed. You cannot do this being bombarded by life.

Principle 3

For a seed to become a tree, it must die. You have to learn discipline.

If you cannot die to things that stop your seed from releasing its gift how will you ever succeed in life?

24 Then Jesus said to His disciples, "If anyone desires to come after Me, let him deny himself, and take up his cross, and follow Me. Matthew 16:24 NKJV

You must learn to die to self, to old friends, old habits, old behaviors, old associations, and old environments. If you do not learn to deny yourself from the things that hinder you, you will never see the real potential of your seed. As long as the person you are continues to live, you cannot become any better. You must die for a new you to be born. The old you and the new you cannot exist at the same time. The only way to accomplish your goals, plans, and aspirations is to become something different. If you could achieve your dreams without being something different, then there would be no need to change. Change comes because you know that in order to accomplish your goals you have to become someone different. Nothing changes until you change. If you refuse to grow then nothing will change in your life, you have to make up your mind. Do you want to become something different or stay the same?

You cannot develop yourself doing nothing you must do something for development to take place. I was always taught that mathematics has to be applied to your life in order for development to take place. If there is no adding and subtracting in your life than you are not changing or becoming any different. What are you adding to your life that is causing you to grow and become more? What are you subtracting from your life that is hindering you from growing and becoming more? If you are poor and choose to stay surrounded by a circle of poor people, tell me how they can help you to become wealthy and influential.

Principle 4

For a seed to become a tree, it must be germinated

You have to find people and things that are going to stretch, develop, and push you. You have to listen to lectures, talks, and find books because they all play a part in germinating you. You have to get around people who make you dream big, think big, and talk big. You have to commit to yourself that after reading this chapter you will be around people who will germinate you.

Principle 5

For a seed to become a tree, you have to water it.

You have to water your seed. That means that you have to develop some habits and routines to do daily to improve yourself. What are you doing on a daily basis to become more? You have to put yourself on some type of plan. I plan monthly to read at least three books and listen to at least five lectures in the area of my gifting. How often are you studying and practicing your area of gifting? My daughter is 15 years old and she has wanted to be an actor since she was five years old. Every week she chooses a monologue out of a movie, she studies the character of that person, and she presents to us the reenactment every Sunday. I have noticed that her doing this has made her become so much greater. She continuously waters her seed. What are you doing to water your seed?

Principle 6

For a seed to become a tree, it has to have fertilizer

You have to refine and refresh yourself on a daily basis to continue growing your seed. You are not going to refine yourself by hanging around people who contaminate you and bring poison into your life. The word of God says,

Don't be fooled by those who say such things, for "bad company corrupts good character." 1 Cor.15:33 NLT

Yea, those around you may be great people, and you may love them, but the direction they have you going in is not a part of your design. Do not allow yourself to be deceived. The people around you are affecting you. You have to put yourself in the midst of people like you who are going for what you are going for so that you can learn and develop. Who are you allowing to fertilize you? People are fertilizer whether you believe it or not. If you continue to hang around bad company and people who are never going anywhere, it will eventually affect you. They will begin to pollute your life, and before you know it, you will be on a path to disaster.

Principle 7

For a seed to become a tree its needs sunshine.

You need an external influence in your life to help you develop your seed into fruit. What seminars have you attended on your seed? What outside influences do you associate with that can help develop your seed? What networks are you a part of that cause your seed to grow? You must have external influences that are outside of your circle of influence so that they can help your seed develop new perspectives.

Principle 8

For a seed to become a tree, it needs time

You need time to develop; you cannot rush what you are to become. It is a process that happens over time. Time helps you develop to the point of greatness. If you were just to jump into who you were designed to become you would miss all the lessons and development that it took to get there along the way. Therefore, your foundation would be so frail that the smallest problems would cause you to collapse. When you lack patience, you look for instant gratification, and when you look for instant gratification, you will always be discouraged because you find out that nothing just happens right away. A seed needs time to bear fruit. Just like the development of you will take time, it does not happen overnight and if you lose sight of that, it could stop your seed from releasing its gift. I know you might not want to continue to do what you are doing. I know you might not want to finish reading this book or study your area of gifting, but if you continue, you will guarantee your own success. Remember to follow the laws of a seed and you will guarantee your success. You must never despise small beginnings because they teach you a lot along the way. Small beginnings help you build a strong foundation because the lessons that you learn on your journey teach you how to withstand the inevitable pressure of life. You will become like a tree that is fully developed; no matter the weather or the season, it stands firm and cannot be removed. That is what you are designed to become when you develop yourself as a tree does, you will be able to deliver your gift. When troubled times come and in the midst of a crisis, you would

not be able to be moved because you are fully developed.

Chapter 6

The Design Of Your Value

The value of every human lies within their gift

Your gift is a natural resource. It is unique, significant, rare and valuable. The gift that proceeds the seed inside you has your value in it. Your success is not outside of you, it is in you. If you genuinely want to become successful, you have to become the person you were designed to be because your value will be found there. Success will always be located in your value because value equals worth and worth equals wealth. Money is attracted to value. If you want to become successful, do not seek success, do not seek to become great, do not seek to become influential and do not seek to become rich and powerful;

only seek to become valuable by becoming who you were designed to be. When you become valuable, wealth, influence, power, and success will find its way to you.

A man's gift makes room for him,
And brings him before great men- Proverbs 18:16 NKJV

Your gift is designed to bring you opportunities and to put you in the presence of powerful people. It is designed to make you stand out from the rest. My gift has lead me, a little boy eating out of government boxes just to survive, to shaking hands with billionaires. Whatever you were designed to do, room will be made available to you. Where your gift is designed to take you, I don't know, but I do know that somewhere you will be in the presence of great people who will take your life to the next level. When you discover, refine and serve your gift success will follow.

When you are valuable success finds you

Diamonds do not look for people, people look for diamonds because diamonds are valuable. Gold does not search for people; people search for gold because gold is valuable. Oil does not dig for people; people dig for oil because oil is valuable. When you become valuable they will look, search and dig for you. You become a person of value when you discover your significant gift to the world and contribute it. You are worth your value. You will find this to be very factual in the market place. The more valuable you are to the marketplace, the more they will pay you. The less valuable you are the less they will pay. They pay you according to your value. If someone helps a company make $100 billion and the companies pay that person $100 million, would that person not be worth it? It is safe to say that that person is valuable. What about the person that makes 10 dollars an hour? It would be safe to say that that person is not that valuable to the marketplace. They may be valuable to their friends and family but not to the marketplace. You will always be paid for your value. People pay for gold because of its value, and people will pay for you because of your value. If you would like to find out if you hold any value on your job, walk into your manager's office and tell them you are resigning, and you will find out quickly if you are valuable or not. If you are valuable, they will try to talk you out of quitting and offer you more money. If you are not valuable, they will gladly let you walk without trying to stop you. The job you are working should be paying you to refine your gift so that one day you become so valuable from refining your gift that they can no longer afford to employ you.

You should not be working only to be employed because you will never become wealthy from a job. You will only become wealthy operating in your gift. Think about all the successful people around you and all the celebrities you see on television, they are operating in their area of gifting. If you are trapped in a job, keep working and you will find out soon enough that your retirement will not be enough to sustain you for the rest of your life. That is why you cannot confuse your work with your job. Your job is what you were trained to do, but your work is your life's purpose which we will discuss in the chapters to come. Your job is your career, but you work is your life's assignment. You will retire from your career one day, but your life's assignment is something that you will never retire from. You will never become wealthy from a job, just pay attention to the people around you at your job and ask yourself, are they wealthy? The answer is probably no, so how do you suppose that you will become wealthy and they started working 10, 20, or 30 years before you did? Only your gift can make you wealthy. You do not want to be like most people who are trapped in a job, struggling just to pay their mortgage and others bills. If you do not catch yourself, you will be trapped in your job forever, struggling to pay your bills. Your gift wants to deploy you because deployment activates your gift, that seed of greatness that the world is looking for. Your seed of greatness is ready to be released. That seed of greatness possesses the hidden value of your life right now, but that value only comes from your focus on refining your seed.

This year alone I have read 30 plus books just to write this book. I had to focus to refine my seed more. I had to narrow my time and discipline myself to completely refine my gift. Now I get paid for taking the time to refine my seed because refining my gift made me valuable. While you are watching television, I am busy reading books in my area of gifting to become refined and more valuable, so they can pay me even more. They will pay you based on your investment in yourself; refine your gift. You are loaded, the gifts you have, the power that you possess, is all trapped in you. After reading this chapter, commit to refining your gift because the only thing that is going to increase your value, is your investment in refining your gift. How many books are you going to buy this month? How many lectures will you listen to this month? How many seminars will you attend this year? How many classes will you take? How many networking events will you go to? What will you do to invest in refining your gift? You have to feed and refine your gift continuously. What are you doing to feed your gift on a daily basis? You have to begin to tap into your gift and refine yourself. People will find you based on how you are feeding and refining your gift. Refining your gift is what creates value. Creating value is a process of refinement. Let's go through that process given by Dr. Myles Munroe:

1. To increase your value, you have to become unique and how do you become unique?

2. You have to become significant and how do you become significant?

3. You have to become rare and how do you become rare?

4. By specializing

Let's dig into the process a little deeper. If you want to increase your value, then you have to become one of a kind. There are a lot of people that do what you do but how are you refining your gift to become the only one doing what you do like you do? This is what you call being unique. Once you learn to become unique, you become sufficiently great at something that no one can ignore, this is called being significant. When you become significant, you become unusually good or remarkable at something and finding another person like you, would be like looking for a needle in a haystack. When people like you are not often found, this is called being rare, and when you are rare, it is because you have become an expert in a particular subject or skill and that my friend is called specializing. Jesus specialized in the impossible like walking on water, raising the dead, healing the sick and restoring sight back to the blind. Those things made people look for him. Those gifts made him valuable because he specialized in during the impossible.

Diamonds, gold, and oil are unique, significant, rare and special. This is why people dig for diamonds, gold, and oil. They are also willing to pay substantial prices for it. When you become unique, significant, and rare, people will pay a hefty price for you. Are you rare or are you just a part of the crowd? The only way you can become rare is by refining your gift. That means you have to work it and work it and work it until it becomes so refined that you become hard to find, you have become rare.

For example, if everyone is selling T-shirts you have to sell a different type of T-shirt, maybe you should design T-shirts for kids. If you sell the same T-shirt as everyone else then you are not rare, you are the same and you do not specialize in anything. You have to find your uniqueness. Do you know why Chick-Fil-A is so big today? It is because they decided not to be like everyone else and sell burgers. They decided to sell nothing but chicken. By doing so,

Chick-Fil-A first became unique, and their uniqueness made them significant, and their significance made them rare because of what they decided to specialize in (CHICKEN).

You must learn to become a specialist in your area of gifting. Decide not to be a 'jack of all trades' but learn to master something. Become a specialist by mastering your gift and success with hunt you down. You must refine what you are best at. If you want to develop your gift, then you have to invest in your gift. You have to invest in books; you have to invest in classes, you have to invest in things that are going to grow your gift. It is going to take investing your time in relationships. You need to only hang around people who can help grow your gift. Investing in your gift will cause you to stop associating with people who cannot grow your gift and who are decreasing your value. If you are spending all your time watching television and hanging out, then you cannot blame anyone but yourself for the value in life, you hold. If you are wondering why you are broke it is because you are not refining your gift, you are not investing in yourself and you are not becoming rare.

Are you not tired of earning a salary? You need people who will pay to get you to stay. You have to become so valuable that you become unaffordable to employ. You become valuable when you specialize. When you begin to specialize, you will lose people because you have to go by yourself. Do not worry about the people who will not go with you, do not worry about the people who will laugh at you sometimes, you have to go by yourself to refine yourself.

In 1996 a young man decided that he wanted to create something rare. He decided that he wanted to create a special T-shirt. He wanted to create a T-shirt that could wick away sweat, keep you cool, dry and that was very light in the cruelest heat conditions. He found something that he wanted to specialize in. At 23 years old, he convinced his former teammates that he played football with at the University of

Maryland to try a T-shirt that he specialized in his grandmother's basement. He also traveled up and down the east coast selling a unique T-shirt out of the trunk of his car. This unique T-shirt resulted in the company we call Under Armour. Kevin Plank became so valuable because he created a product that was unique. No one else had anything like this on the market which made him significant, and he became significant because he created something rare. Everyone was selling t-shirts, including Kevin himself, but what set him apart from all the others selling T-shirts was that he decided to create a special T-shirt he chose to be unique. You have to learn to specialize because specializing in something will bring you wealth.

You have to master your gifts. Remember, for you to become valuable you have to specialize. Your value is in your specialization; this is why you have to work to refine your gift, so that you become one of a kind, we call this being 'special'.

Chapter 7

Designed By The Way You Think

If you truly believe in your heart, you were designed in a specific way that will allow you to succeed in the area of your gift, then your thoughts will forge into reality what your mind believes.

What you are designed to become will be affected by the way you think. Everything you have inside of you will remain trapped if your thoughts are trapped. The way you think is ultimately responsible for what you become. The way you think can lead you away from your design. Where you currently are in life is based on the way you have been conditioned to think. If you have been conditioned to think in a successful way you will become successful, but if you have been conditioned to think you will fail then chances are, you will fail. The condition of your thoughts determine the condition of your life. If you want to change the condition of your life, you have to change the condition of your thoughts. You will never lose weight having the same mindset about food and exercising that you have always had. Your thoughts are the most powerful resource you have. You can have all the talent in the world but if your thoughts do not allow you to operate in the capacity of your design, your gifts and talents will mean nothing.

All that you are designed to become will be a direct result of how you think. Yes, you are engineered to become something wonderful, but your ability to achieve great things in life lies within the power of your thoughts.

We demolish arguments and every pretension that sets itself up against the knowledge of God, and we take captive every thought to make it obedient to Christ." (2 Cor.10:5) NIV

There is a war going on in our mind; that war is fought daily. The war is between the thoughts entering our mind that come from the enemy and thoughts that come from our divine Father. God is concerned with the way we think because he knows the way we think determines what we become. We have been given the power and ability through the holy spirit to capture every thought that exalts itself above what God designed us to become. We can block and dispose them from having any effect on our lives. God does not want us to be prisoners of a negative way of thinking. He does not want us being prisoners of thoughts that cause us to become something we were never designed to be. He wants us to take every negative thought and submit it to him. Then ask the Holy Spirit to cleanse the deceitful thought from our mind and enable us to be alert to anything that tries to destroy our design.

Your life is a reflection of your thoughts

Your thought determines how you feel, and how you feel determines the decisions you make. The decisions you make determine your actions, and your actions determine your habits. Your habits determine your character and your character determines your destination in life. The moment you think you are not designed to become something is the moment you begin to feel that way. Once you start feeling that way, you begin to make decisions based on how you feel. Those decisions lead to actions that lead you away from becoming what you are designed to be. Those actions lead to habits that create a character that is not you. Once you become something, you are not, you arrive at a place that is not designed for you to succeed. If you want to change your destination in life, you have to change your character. In order to change your character, you have to change your habits. To change your habits, you have to change your actions. To change your actions, you have to change your decisions. To change your decisions, you have to change the way you feel. To change the way you feel, you have to change your thoughts. Your life is a reflection of your thoughts. The reality that you are currently shaping in your thoughts is determining your future. Everything you experience in your world has originated from your thoughts.

For example, three men were digging a hole and as they dig they were asked the question.

What are you doing?

The first man replied digging up dirt.

The second man replied working to pay my bills.

The third man replied building a water well that will permit thousands of people to drink clean water and eliminate diseases caused by bacteria from dirty water.

The first man saw nothing, the second man saw a way to pay his bills, and the third person saw what the project was designed to become. He saw the work as it will be not as it was. He saw the benefits that it will bring to people. He saw a finished product. Who do you think had the better mindset? All three people are doing the same thing, but only one could see the finished product.

Your thoughts will always interpret what you see and hear

The power of your mind will cause you to have a different experience than the person sitting right next to you. What a person sees and hears is small compared to how he or she thinks. The way someone thinks determines what they see and hear. Their perception of a thing is based on their thoughts. Your thoughts will always interpret what you see and hear. Many time people think that their circumstances control the way they feel, not knowing that the way they think has created the circumstance. The problems, the struggles, and current situations all reflect your mindset. You are where you are because of your thoughts whether they are wanted or unwanted. Your thought power creates your reality.

When I managed a group of sales people, I would give out performance bonuses. Some would be excited, and others would be disappointed. I did not get it at the time but thinking back, I understand why some would be excited and why others would not be. Every one of them began at the same starting line but in that room, were those who thought they could win the bonus money and those who thought they could not. The ones who thought they could win were excited about bonus money. Those who thought they could not win would leave the meeting being negative. Your thoughts interpret your reality.

The success that you wish to see right now is at your disposal, but you must learn to align your thinking with who you were designed to become.

If a great opportunity smacked a negative person in the face, they would still think negatively about it because they got smacked. The cup will be half full or half empty based on your thoughts. I never look at a problem as a problem. I look at it as an opportunity to grow and develop. It will not be a problem if I know how to fix it before it becomes a problem. It is a problem because it is there to teach me something I do not know. It is there to stretch me. That is how I think of every issue. I know there are millions of people out there that would not dare think this way, and those my friend, are the people who never get ahead in life. Inside you are dormant abilities beyond your imagination but they are only accessible through your thought life. The success that you wish to see right now is at your disposal, but you must learn to align your thinking with who you are designed to become. A great friend of mine has a kid that is about to enter the NFL draft. His name is Dylan Dawkins. Though-out life Dylan's abilities have been challenged. He was always told he was too small to play running back and that he would not be successful if he continued trying to play that position. So many people thought he would not make it, but at every level, from elementary to college, he has proven them wrong. Never once did he think he was too small. Dylan would go head to head with people twice his size and make it through them. No matter what they thought about him, he never thought negatively about himself. That is why he has succeeded at every level and I have no doubt that he will in the NFL. He thinks different. I remember people constantly saying those exact words to me in the workplace. They would say "you are not like the others". When they spoke those words, I knew they really meant that I thought differently than others around me.

You must choose to think different

Those who you see on television or read about in magazines all thought differently than the people around them. In order to become different, you have to think different. If everyone around you thinks negatively, you will be no different. I made it out of poverty, out of the projects, and did not become a statistic because I thought differently. I remember my mother traveling to churches to get boxes of food so that we would have food to eat. I thought at that moment in my life, as a young boy, that if I ever had kids they would never have to endure what I had to. I never thought like the people around me. I always thought differently. Some of the friends I grew up with are dead or in prison for the remainder of their life. They chose not to think different. I made it out because I did. I know that you cannot hear the passion in my voice at the moment, but if you are reading or listening to this book, I am telling you that it is possible for you to think different in an environment that tries to condition you to think you will never make it out. If I can become successful and climb out of a hole so deep, filled with poverty, you too can. Since I thought different, I was able to change the course of my life. You have to start thinking about what you think about, or you will hold the very person you are designed to become. Your thoughts become a reality.

Everything you lay eyes on in this world originated from someone's mind. They saw it in their thoughts and then made it a reality. To become what you were designed to be, you must learn to control the nature of your dominating thoughts. Doing this will attract what you wish to see in your life but not doing this will attract the things you hate the most. Everything you desire to come true in your life is only a thought away. All you have to do is think it into existence. Every thought you think is either shaping your life the way you want or shaping a life that you will despise. Either way, your thoughts are forging your reality.

I was during some research online and came across a case study done by Psychologists, Ulrich Weger and Stephen Loughnan. The case study involves two groups of people answering their questions. The people in one group were told that before each question, the answer would quickly flash on their screen. It would flash too quickly for them to consciously perceive, but slow enough for their unconscious to take in. The other group was told that the flashes simply signaled the next question. But in all actuality for both groups, a random string of letters where flashed across their screens not the answers. But the people who thought the answers were flashed did better on the test. Expecting to know the answer made people more likely to get the answer right. When you cause your mind to believe something, it tries to forge that belief into reality. If you sincerely believe that you were designed in a way to succeed in your area of gifting, then your thoughts will forge into reality what your mind believes. When your mind believes something, it causes your thoughts to create actions and those actions, compel you to behave in a certain way that will begin shaping into reality what you believe.

Be aware of fraudulent thoughts

Well, you might be saying to yourself, if it was that easy, why isn't everyone successful? I am sure no one starts out in life believing they can't do something, and you are right. Once the mind believes it can achieve something, a fraudulent thought comes along that destroys that belief. There is a fraud that exists within your thoughts that is trying to shape a reality of its own. He is there to steal your dreams, to kill your confidence, and dismantle your hope. He is the silent voice that whispers in your thoughts that you do not have what it takes. You are not going to make it. What makes you think you can do that? You are not smart enough. You cannot start your own business. No one is going to give you an opportunity. You do not have enough talent. No one is going to like you. You are going to fail. You are never going to succeed. Why try this and you know it is not going to work? He is the fraud that instills fear into your life helping you form negative thoughts about what you are designed to become.

The fraud in your mind is a parasite. Those fraudulent thoughts eat away at every positive thought. They destroy your excitement and energy. They eat away at your desire to accomplish something great. The fraud's job is to make sure your thought life remains negative. As a matter of fact, it feeds on negativity. It loves for you to hang around people that discourage you. Those fraudulent thoughts are there to make you second guess yourself. Those thoughts are there to constantly remind you that you do not have the experience. That people are not going to be satisfied with your services and that you lack the ability to become something you are not. To stop the fraud from destroying your life you have to become aware when it is speaking to you. You have to know that the moment you believe in something, right behind that belief is the fraud. You must not allow those fraudulent thoughts to talk you out of what you believe. Recognize when it speaks and silence it right away by stating out loud that I can, and I will move forward on what I believe. The more you continue to speak out loud what you believe, the fraud will disappear from your thought life. It is very important to guard your thought life because in those thoughts exists everything you are to become.

Your thoughts can place limitations on your design

You cannot allow your thoughts to set limitations on what you can become. I have watched so many people who are amazingly gifted permit their thoughts to limit the expansion of their abilities. It is like their thoughts convince them that they are only good using their gifts in certain areas, when they have the abilities to use them far beyond the limits they place on themselves. Those people allow their secondary thoughts to tell them they will not be good at doing something they were designed to do. They have the gift to do it, but their thoughts convinced them not to operate outside of their comfort zone. When you do not allow yourself to jump into new things that make you uncomfortable, your thoughts become the limitation to all that you can become. You can never know what you can grow to be if you do not travel down all the roads that are

131

connected to your gift/s. If it is a part of your design and you are naturally gifted at it, yet you do not allow yourself to do it because your thoughts create a fear of failing or getting uncomfortable then you my friend are limiting yourself. The only way to lift the limitations your mind places on you, is to do something different, to do something that you have never tried before, and to do something uncomfortable as long as it is in your area of gifting. Try something out of the norm that allows you to use your gift and operate within your design.

Let this mind be in you which was also in Christ Jesus, 6 who, being in the form of God, did not consider it robbery to be equal with God, 7 but made Himself of no reputation, taking the form of a bondservant, and coming in the likeness of men. Philippians 2:5-6 NKJV

Notice in the above text that it suggested that you think as Christ thought. So how did Christ think? The word of God said that he thought that being equal to God would not be robbing God of who he is. He suggested that we think the same way. You should not consider it taking anything away from God by placing yourself equal to him. You are equal to God, you were created in his image and likeness. I did not say it, the scripture did. Therefore, since you are equal to God, then you can call those things that do not exist into existence. Christ never thought anything was impossible. The word of God wants you to think the same way. What you are to become is not impossible you just have to think it is possible.

Your brain gives birth to what it can conceive

What you are designed to become is first conceived in the mind. Everything that you will become will be born out of your mind. Conception must take place in your mind before your design can make it a reality. Once you start thinking, conception begins to take place and conception, once conceived in the mind gives birth to a brainchild. Microsoft is Bill Gates brainchild. It was born out of his mind. Ford Motor Co. is Henry Ford's brainchild, it was born out of his mind. Google is Larry Page and Sergey Brin's brainchild, it was born out of their minds. What brainchild are you giving birth to? What you are to become is conceived in your mind. You can never give birth to something your mind never designs. Your mind is the designer of your future. What you want to become, what you want to do and what you want to accomplish is all designed in your mind.

Chapter 8

Vision Of Design

Who you are to become, only becomes clear
when you can see beyond your current reality.

Walt Disney was fired from a newspaper because he "lacked imagination and had no good ideas." Steven Spielberg was rejected from film school, not once...not twice...but three times. Bill Belichick was fired as the head coach of the Cleveland Browns because the owners believed he could not take them to the Super Bowl. Oprah Winfrey, at the age of 22, was fired from her job as a television reporter because she was told she was "unfit for TV". What led these successful and gifted people to continue in the face of failure and rejection?

They saw what they were created to become. They saw a mental picture of their future. They saw their future self. They saw what they were but had not yet become. They saw something that extended beyond their reality, that created an image, that showed them what they were but had not yet become. This we call vision.

What is vision

Vision is the thing that brings a glimpse of the future into your life. Vision is the thing that helps unleash your potential (the real you). Vision creates a longing to develop and grow. It gives us an expectation of who we are to become. It chooses your future. What you become in time is determined by what you can imagine now. There was an unknown actor in the early 1990s, that was struggling to make ends meet. While struggling he imagined himself not as he was but as he would be. He decided to write himself a check for $10 million for "acting services rendered," dated it for 1994 and carried it in his wallet for daily inspiration. In 1994, Jim

Carrey learned he would reap exactly $10 million for his role in Dumb and Dumber. Today, Carrey is one of America's top movie stars — and he credits his constant visualization with helping him get there.

Where there is no vision, the people perish: but he that keepeth the law, happy is he.
-Proverbs 29-18

Vision starts the activity

Vision is what gives the architect its blueprint. Vision is a picture that one has in the mind whether it's about self, business or any other future endeavors. It is the thing that compels you to search for a greater version of yourself. Once you can see beyond your current reality, you gain clarity of your dreams. Clearness of a vision will help you achieve goals, produce more and become who you are not yet. Vision plays a vital part in learning who you are designed to become. When you are able to see what you can become, you feel much more valuable as a person. The more you become what you see, the more valuable you become in life. In essence, vision increases your value.

Why is vision so vital to becoming

Why is vision so important to becoming? The answer is so, so simple. When you are unable to see beyond what you currently are, how can you become something different? It is the ability to see the future picture of yourself that helps you focus on exactly what you want to become. The picture of the future makes becoming who you were born to be easier and faster. It brings what does not exist into existence. Anything that has ever been created started in the mind of someone. It was not physical; it had no form or reality. Vision is the power that takes a thing from non-existence and makes it a reality. Everything God created he first saw. God saw the light before it existed. He saw the stars, the sun, and moon before it existed. Everything that we experience on planet earth came out of God. God pulled out of himself everything he saw. Vision pulls our focus together like a magnet, and it attracts and connects all that we need to become. When we focus our brain on what we want, we increase the amount of the cellular rhythm of our mind, body, and soul.

Vision is so vital that it affects all aspects of your life; emotionally, physically, mentally and corporately. When you see a picture of your future self, it helps you overcome obstacles and hold on when times get tough. That is because vision helps you to focus on the future when you live in the present. Therefore, you can go through tough times because you know that where you are and what you are going through is not your future. When you are convinced by your vision that where you are is temporary, it gives you the ability to smile in the midst of any trouble or unwanted situation. Vision makes it possible to smile on your Job when you hate it because you know that the job is not a part of your future.

Vision helps you picture yourself in the future. Those pictures create purpose, purpose creates drive, and drive brings success. Vision helps you discover who you will become, without it you have no blueprint on what to be, what to do, or how to succeed. Having no vision will cause a lack of drive and passion and you will just go with the flow of life. Vision activates your passion and causes your potential to pour out of you like a waterfall. Vision helps guide you into what you are to become and why you are becoming it. Vision will keep you motivated and driven to find your true self. It helps you focus in a way that brings the things you see and want in life into reality. It helps you see a better future. It makes you more productive and happier. It gives you the ability to will things into being. The greater the vision or the further you see yourself in the future, the more changes you will make to accomplish what it is that you see.

The starting point of your vision should be emotional, physical, and intellectual. When vision becomes established, it becomes a fundamental key to success during your journey through life. Vision establishes your victory or defeat on how, when, where and what you receive and possess.

When people begin to see with their mind and heart, they change their world

The more you start to become what you see, the more potential you force out of you. The more you and your vision become intertwined, you stop seeing with the naked eye but instead you start to see with your mind and heart. When people begin to see with their mind and heart, they change their world. Lindsey Vonn, one of the most successful female skiers in history, the gold medalist, says her mental practice gives her a competitive advantage on the course. In many interviews, including one with MindBodyGreen, she stated that "I always visualize the run before I do it. By the time I get to the start gate, I've run that race 100 times already in my head, picturing how I'll take the turns." But she doesn't just keep the images in her head. She is also known to physically simulate the path by literally shifting her weight back and forth as if she were on skis, as well as practice the specific breathing patterns she will use during the race. "I love that exercise," Vonn has said. "Once I visualize a course, I never forget it. So, I get on those lines and go through exactly the run that I want to have."

Vision is so powerful that it can determine the outcome in every situation. Vision makes the future predictable. If you see yourself winning, you never lose. If you see yourself successful, you become it. The problem is that must people do not see anything. Therefore, they become nothing. You have to see something before you can become it. My life today is a reflection of my vision. I used to be in the car business. I remember this particular time when I no longer wanted to be a salesman. Instead, I wanted a promotion to become a Finance Manager. Every night when everyone left and went home, I would go into one of the finance managers offices and picture myself in front of a customer doing the work they did. Not long after that, I become a finance manager. Everything I have ever accomplished in life, I saw myself doing it first. Everyone of my visions has helped me predict my future. I saw it, and it became a reality.

Make a mental picture in your mind, add feelings and emotions to that mental image. Then picture what it is that you desire, see yourself giving every step to its completion, give thanks like you have received it already and keep the emotions parallel to the vision. That vision will become reality and manifest something far beyond your wildest dreams. Having a vision demands persistence and discipline.

Visionaries live in the future

In order to become what you are designed to be, you must first see it. Becomers have the ability to see today as it is and calculate a future that continuously grows. Arnold Schwarzenegger once stated that he had a fixed idea of growing a body like Reg Park's. He stated, "the model was there in my mind; I only had to grow enough to fill it". He then added "the more I focused in on this image and worked and grew, the more I saw it was real and possible for me to be like him." Later, when he transitioned to a career in acting and politics, Schwarzenegger said he employed similar mental tricks: "It's the same process I used in bodybuilding: What you do is create a vision of who you want to be — and then live that picture as if it were already true."

A successful becomer can see the future and still stay focused on the present. Those on their way to becoming, see a vision, not as a dream, but a reality that has not come into existence yet. A vision is easily perceived for becomers because their levels of commitment and sureness for what they see are so clear. Abraham had a problem becoming who he was designed to be because he could not see clear. Take a look at these verses in Genesis

After these things the word of the Lord came to Abram in a vision, saying, "Do not be afraid, Abram. I am your shield, your exceedingly great reward."
2 But Abram said, "Lord God, what will You give me, seeing I go childless, and the heir of my house is Eliezer of Damascus?" 3 Then Abram said, "Look, You have given me no offspring; indeed one born in my house is my heir! And behold, the word of the Lord came to him, saying, "This one shall not be your heir, but one who will come from your own body shall be your heir." 5 Then He brought him outside and said, "Look now toward heaven, and count the stars if you are able to number them." And He said to him, "So shall your descendants be." –Genesis 15:1- 5 NKJV

Did you take note of what Abraham saw? The text said he saw himself childless. He did not see himself as a father. He did not see a child in his future. He did not see a child calling him father. All he could see was the fact that he was childless and could not bear any children. God knew that if he could not get Abraham to see himself as a father of many nations, he would never become it. So, God told

Abraham to go outside and count the stars. That way every time Abraham walked outside and saw the stars it would remind him of the offspring he would have. God began to affect his vision so that he could see what he was designed to become. God had to give Abraham a vision so that it could become a reality. Abraham would have never become a father of many nations unless he first saw it. You have to see your future first, or you will never get there. Becomers live in the future. Becomers spend hours upon hours bringing into reality what does not exist. Their vision becomes a dominant force driving them to action.

All Things Are Possible Within A Vision

To establish that type of drive and passion, you will need to know precisely what you want the future you to look like. Question yourself about your future. What does the future you look like? Is the future you a teacher, singer, tech inventor, engineer, actor, author, CEO, dancer, movie producer, manager, speaker, or just someone who wants to affect the world. Tell yourself specifically how you picture your life. All things are possible in a vision. When you build your vision, build it great. When you create a successful vision, you begin to activate a strong urge; a deep feeling called passion. The only way to be efficient in your vision is to imagine what you can become and set goals and a plan of action to reach your vision which we will talk about in the chapters to come.

The purpose of this book is to help you to start becoming so that you begin to discover more parts of you that you did not know existed. It is important to identify precisely who you are right now in order to see who you want to become. This includes your lifestyles, habits, attitudes, and points of view. Take a moment to gain a clear summary of yourself so that you can begin to discover the future you. When you can locate the future you in your imagination, riches beyond your wildest dreams in every area of your life shall become yours.

How to establish a clear vision

Everybody ends up somewhere in life. A few people end up somewhere on purpose. Those are the people with vision, with a clearly defined dream.

Practice Your Vision On A Daily Basis

Practice your vision on a daily basis by setting aside at least 10 to 15 minutes a day to picture your vision; a picture of the future you. Act out in your mind the vision you would like to achieve, talk to yourself like you have achieved it, and you will begin to bring what you are designed to become to life. If you take the time to imagine the future you daily, I promise you will see its manifestation. All you have to do is see the picture and God will provide the resources. As a becomer, acting on your vision will provide you with the focus needed to accomplish your goals. Vision helps becomers work on what is essential.

Vision Creates Light That Shines On A Dark Path

Without a vision, you are in complete darkness. When you sit down and plan how you are going to make your vision a reality, it will suddenly become daylight, and the sun will shine brightly on an unknown path called life. It will enable you to see for miles around you, and that is when it will be the time to travel an unfamiliar path. Your true vision will always be tested for authenticity. The vision you have will make sure you are serious and real. Things in life will come your way to test your vision. Things that you expect to happen will not happen. Disappointment after disappointment will take place. You will lose friends and the people who you thought were there to support you. Distractions will come along that will try to steer you off course. You must hold tight to the vision that you want to become a reality. When the vision you see is still standing amidst all the adversity you have faced, your vision will be authentic and once this happens, you will obtain everything you saw. Strong vision inspires passion and that passion transforms and creates change in your life.

Chapter 9

Recognize Your Passion

It is obvious that we can no more explain a passion
to a person who has never experienced it than we
can explain light to the blind." – T.S. Elliot

Passion is what defines the very emotional essence

of our being. It is what activates our reason to make an

impact, and contribution to our world. Passion drives our

motivation; it inspires us to forge into reality who we are

designed to become.

Passion is that intense drive that illuminates our path

toward aggressively achieving our purpose in life. Passion is

an aggressive emotion; it instils the need to be bold,

courageous, and fearless. Passion gives us drive, but more

than that, it makes us feel that the world we live in is waiting for our contribution. Being passionate is not just about knowing, it is also about feeling. That is what makes passion so important; it makes us feel that we are on the right path in life and gives us confidence and hopes which continues to stir our vision toward our future.

Passionate people are emotional, but all emotional people are not passionate. Passion brings out activity while emotion brings only feelings. An emotional person becomes affected by their feelings while passionate people get inspired, creative and bold. Passionate people do not allow their feelings to control them. Passionate people commit to a vision and actions that will help them to accomplish their why. Passionate people do not complain, they figure out how to do something about the very thing they do not like. That is why people who hate their lives are not passionate, but instead they are emotional. Hatred for something fuels a passionate person, it makes them angry until they can change it. Passionate people have this conviction in them that makes them believe they can change the impossible.

Passion demands take over

When you embrace your passion, it takes over and does things that challenge and stretch you. It drives limits, destroys traditions and eventually, redesigns your world. To strive for your passion is to be different from the rest. Passion is an internal drive that keeps you going no matter what.

There was a Junior School teacher who got so inspired one day by her passion that she quit her job as a public-school teacher to become a missionary teacher. She did not go to a private Catholic school where she could earn more money. Instead, she decided that she wanted to be a missionary teacher of one of the poorest cities in our world today, Calcutta (which is now known as Kolkata, the capital of the Indian state of West Bengal). Every time she went to school she walked through a place that you and I would probably call hell on earth. The path she walked every day was filled with disease and people lying dead in the mud with flies attaching themselves to the bodies repeatedly; she walked over bodies that died during the night and saw people's legs rotting. She wept every day she went to class until one day she became so angry that she brought action to the situation. She became convicted by things she was experiencing.

Find your conviction

The conviction within her stirred up hatred in her heart, and that hatred turned into anger. Something has to make you angry. Until you are angry, you have not discovered a reason to become what you were designed to be. On the road to becoming you have to become aware of what makes you angry. Passion makes you angry because it gets you to the point where you cannot take something anymore. The teacher quit her job to care for the poor but before resigning from her job she had to obtain permission from her supervisor. He expressed his thoughts about her quitting and tried to talk her out of it, but there was no way that he could. She asked for her last paycheck and left to go spend it all at the market. She brought fruits and veggies. She took it and gave it to the people on the open street and that day, Mother Teresa was born.

Usually, when people are sad, they don't do anything. They just cry over their condition. But when they get angry, they bring about a change." - Malcolm X

When you embrace your passion as Mother Teresa did, it takes over and does things that challenge and stretch you. As I said before, it drives limits, destroys traditions and eventually redesigns your world. To strive for your passion is to be different from the rest. Mother Teresa was not the only person to travel that road every day, but she was the only one that allowed her passion to become a conviction.

When you have uneasiness and restlessness in your heart for something you believe, then you have a conviction and a conviction is necessary on your journey to becoming who you were designed to be. It moves you toward an emotion that resembles anger. It is an intense feeling that speaks to you until you begin to move toward an action to satisfy your beliefs. Martin Luther King Jr. acted on his conviction. Gandhi acted on his conviction. Rosa Parks acted on her conviction. They would not have affected the world if they had not acted on their conviction. A conviction is the only kind of belief that will move you to sacrifice your life. When you are willing to die for something you believe in, no one can stop you. When you are willing to die to become what you are designed to be then nothing will prevent you from becoming it. Martin Luther King Jr, Gandhi, Rosa Parks, Nelson Mandela and Jesus were all willing to die for what they believed they had to become to contribute to their generation. What is your conviction about who you are going to become?

Passion does not allow you to become average

Passion will never allow you to do things at a moderate level. Passion causes you to go all out, to the point where people begin to call you reckless and crazy. I can just imagine all the bad press Mother Teresa got on her journey to making a difference in the lives of the poverty-stricken people of Calcutta. I know many people told her that it would be foolish and a big waste of her time to help change the reality of poverty-stricken people. However, when you are passionate about something it cannot be turned off or turned down. It does not stop until it becomes what it knows it can be. Passion enables us to live with an intent to make an impact that will bring about change. It fuels our motivation and inspires us to create opportunities for a better destiny (for us or for those we care for). Passion is what defines our entity.

Passion is what inspired Wendy Kopp to found Teach For America. It is a diverse network of leaders who confront educational inequity through teaching and working with an unwavering commitment from every sector of society to create a nation free from injustice. While going for a Bachelor of Arts at Princeton University, she discovered that there was a severe disparity in the educational system in the United States. She became so moved by this discovery that she decided to make this the focus of her thesis. While doing research and writing her thesis she found that there was a shortage of teachers and a push to get college graduates on wall street, but no push to fix the inequity and injustice in our country's educational system. She recognized that if she did not play a part in changing the realm of inequity in the education system, that it would continue to drive poverty, racism, crime and other rooted injustices that came from a lack of a proper education, even higher. Her passion motivated her to do something to change the injustice in the educational system. She has been quoted saying that when the idea came to her head that she could change a country's problem, she obsessed about it day and night, that her thesis became her blueprint for her plan to change the inequality of the educational system. So, in 1989 in her own words in an interview with National Public Radio, she stated.

"Well, in the last week of writing the thesis, I decided, I'm just going to say to my professor in the thesis that I'm going to go do this. So, he liked the idea, but he thought it was really crazy to think that I was really going to try to go do this. So, I had this plan. And one of the things I had looked at was the origin of the Peace Corps. And there's this incredible paper, and in that paper, was this beautiful analysis that concluded that it had to start with 500 core members, that was the smallest possible number that would seem nationally important, but that it was a workable number. Anything bigger would be unmanageable. So that became my number. Like, OK, we've got to recruit 500 people."

Passion is found when you are so moved emotionally by a problem in the lives of others that you know you can do something about

The whole plan was to inspire thousands of people to apply in the first year, and select, and train and place no fewer than 500 of them in, you know, five or six communities across the country. And I had a budget saying, this was going to cost $2.5 million in the first year. And my thesis advisor became really obsessed with that number. Like, how are you going to raise $2.5 million? And he said, you know, do you know how hard it is to raise $2,500? And he sat me down. He said, I'll tell you what. I'm going to link you up with the head of development at Princeton who's going to explain how hard it is to raise $2,500." When you are moved by a passion, the word impossible does not register in your heart or mind. Impossible is something that never comes to your mind. People with passion intend to do things that are impossible. Even though her professor called her deranged for thinking that she could do the impossible. Wendy left his office and did the impossible. She raised 2.5 million dollars and recruited and trained 489 college graduates without having any training or teaching experience. Passion is what will lead a person to impact a country. Passion is an internal drive that keeps you going no matter what. That is why the only people who keep going after being knocked down many times are the passionate ones. Passion allows one to go through all the obstacles that try to stop them from reaching who they were designed to become.

In 1993, a young woman became jobless, divorced, penniless and a single parent. She had no way to provide for her child so she went on government-assisted welfare. While constantly being knocked down by life she never stopped working on her passion. Two years later, she finished the manuscript for her book. She sent it out to 12 different major publishers, and they all rejected her book. But because of her passion, she persisted, and a year later, a small publisher gave her a small advance of £1500 and published just 1000 copies of her book.

J.K Rowling has sold more than 400 million copies of her Harry Potter books and is worth more than $1 billion today.

Les Brown stated that

"Wanting something is not enough. You must hunger for it. Your motivation must be absolutely compelling in order to overcome the obstacles that will invariably come your way."

Life is filled with things waiting to activate your passion because it is the only thing that can make you believe you can change the world. It is the thing that lets you know you are living to make a difference. Deep down inside of every human is a desire not just to exist but to make a contribution with the life they were given.

I was watching a movie a while back called The Family That Preys. One of the characters in the movie, Charlotte, stated to Alice "Are you living or are you existing?" People do not live they just exist. They go with the flow of life, follow trends, chase the crowd and live reactively to their environment. Nobody takes the time to find out or become who they are. Instead, I watch people lock who they are, what they love and want to do in a box to pretend to be something they are not, just to be accepted. People work jobs they hate, do things they don't like, buy stuff they don't want and hang out with people they don't really like. The only way for you to live is to do something that is connected to your passion.

Start a business, record music, write a book, create an app, become an actor, designer, model, or world leader because after all, this is what your heart aches for, everything else is just a distraction in your life.

Bill Gates was so passionate about software in computers that he created Microsoft, but before he created Microsoft, he was an inexperienced computer programmer who had a passion for writing computer code. That passion was so strong that in the eighth grade, he managed to get excused from math class to design things like the first video games. When the passion in you is active, you will notice it because these signs will become a part of your life.

How to recognize when you are passionate about something

You will begin to sleep less, which is actually not a good thing but, passion will have you so excited about what you are doing that you will go to bed late thinking about the thing that stirs your passion, and that same excitement will get you out of bed early. Passionate people are all about doing something that fuels their passion to the point that they ca not sleep.

You will find you are passionate about something when you become obsessed

When you are operating in something you are passionate about you will not be able to keep your mind from constantly thinking about it because of the excitement it brings to your heart. Passion keeps people trapped in a world of their own and this causes them to bend the world to what they believe. Most all charismatic and magnetic people live by following their deep passion.

You will find you are passionate about something when you get angry about it

You are extremely and emotionally connected to the thing/s you are passionate about. My wife is so passionate about beauty, style, and make-up that when she sees an actor or host on Television and their style is off, or make-up or hair is done in an incorrect way, she gets so twisted inside, and she does not even recognize or know the person.

You will find you are passionate about something when you are willing to risk it all

Passionate people go all out for the thing/s they cannot live without. That is why passionate people are willing to gamble there who life savings and everything they have to fulfill their passion.

You will find you are passionate about something because you never stop working

Passion is not just an emotional feeling, but it is who and what you are. For a passionate person to stop working would be like him/her no longer being themselves. When you are operating in your passion, you never work because doing what you love is a part of your nature. Doing what you love is doing what makes you, You.

You will find you are passionate about something when you can't stop talking about it

Everyone hates talking to you because they know once they get you going, the thing that you are passionate about will not stop pouring out of your mouth. After all, when you are passionate about something what else is there to talk about?

You will find you are passionate about something because you stop living in the present.

Passionate people are so far ahead in their mind that the present is just a moment in time and the future is where they live. What's next is always on their mind. Once you have found your passion, you will find characteristic traits in you that you did not know existed, but those traits are there because they reflect your passion. Passion designs a new being, a new person, someone you have not seen before. Mother Teresa was moved by the condition of the poor in her community and it compelled her to become someone she never saw before.

J.K Rowling was moved by a story that she wanted to tell kids and it compelled her to become someone she never saw before.

Wendy Kopp was moved by the inequalities of the U.S educational system and it compelled her to become someone she never saw before.

Bill Gates was moved by his abilities to change personal computing and it compelled him to become someone different.

What are you moved by that will compel you to become someone you never saw?

The ultimate example of passion was that of Jesus Christ. No one can ever dispute the passion of Jesus Christ. He had conviction rooted so deep that it allowed him to take on suffering beyond what we can really imagine. If you were to read through the gospels of Matthew, Mark, Luke, and John, you will find a lot about the passion of Christ and how he was moved with compassion for humanity.

Luke 9:22 says 'For I, the Son of Man, must suffer many terrible things,' he said. 'I will be rejected by the leaders, the leading priests, and the teachers of religious law. I will be killed, but three days later I will be raised from the dead'" (NLT).

He willingly took on this experience, for those with hatred for him and those with love for him. What human being could do what he did? There have been many great leaders willingly die for what they believe but how many of them would be willing to suffer what Christ suffered for people who would ultimately crucify him? Only Jesus, with the strength of the father, was able to follow through knowing about the pain and torture he would endure for the sake of humanity. The Passion and conviction pushed him and he knew that if he did not go through with it, then the forgiveness for our sins would never come to pass. That passion kept him motived and driven to accomplish his goal; the forgiveness of sins for all humanity. The passion that lead Jesus to die on that cross for us, gives me a feeling of love that I cannot explain. It stirs in me a passion so strong that makes me want to go hard for him every day. Thank you, Jesus, for what you did for every one of us on the cross of Calvary. I can say without a shadow of doubt I know that God loves me.

Chapter 10

You Must Plan To Become

Planning is bringing the future into the present so that you can do something about it now - Alan Lakein

Now that you have formed a mental picture of your future and you understand that passion will be your driving force, you must now plan to get there. Vision helps you see your future in pictures which allow you to establish a foundation; having a plan will build the house. Vision lays the foundation, but plans do the building. Take a look at the houses around you and know that before those houses were built, someone had to see it there first. Seeing the house creates the foundation, but the house will not become a reality with visualization the only activity that must take over the vision. This is what we call a plan; it is the activity. Vision is the key ingredient because without the vision nothing can be planned and if nothing is planned, then no future can be built. That's why your life is determined by the plans you have. The outcomes that you want to experience in life are built on the plans that you have and do not have. If you do not plan to succeed, then you plan to fail. Your success in life will be found in the plans you have. You have to plan to become who you were designed to be. Planning gets successful people where they are. Who you are and what you are to become will only happen with a plan. A motion does not happen unless there is movement. How can you expect a better future if you do not plan it?

You have to plan your success

There was a bright young man that planned the success of his future while in elementary school. As a child in elementary he planned to become an entrepreneur. He started out working in his grandfather's grocery store to create some working capital to invest. He took that money he earned from his grandfather's grocery store and all of the other jobs to buy some stock. At 11 years old, he made his first investment, buying three shares of Cities Service Preferred at $38 per share. By the age of 13, he starts a few businesses. He sold cold drinks, weekly magazines, stamps, chewing gum and went door to door delivering newspapers, and even began selling his own horseracing tip sheets. That same year he filed a tax return on all of the income he earned and used his bicycle as a write-off. His investing continued into high school.

During his time in high school, he partnered up with a friend and the two bought a pinball machine and installed it in a barbershop. That pinball machine generated enough income to buy another two pinball machines that they installed in barbershops. They eventually sold the business for $1200. His interest in investing and plans to become wealthy did not stop there. He went on to college to earn a

Master of Science in Economics. After that, he went on to sell securities for Buffett-Falk & Company for three years, then worked for his mentor for two years as an analyst at Graham-Newman Corp. While working for his mentor, he formed a firm called Buffett Partnership Ltd in his hometown. Utilizing the methods, he learned from his mentor Benjamin Graham, leads him to become successful identifying undervalued companies. That ability translated into millions. Thus, becoming the person today, you know as Warren Buffett.

Plans are the roadmap, they help you see where you are going and how to get there

Everything Warren Buffett has become he chose to become by planning to become it. A plan will map out things you must do to achieve the life you want, as well as the things you must not do in order to accomplish the life you want. If you have a vision with no plan then how do you expect the images you see of your future to become reality?

Let me let you in on a little secret. Nothing just happens, let me repeat it, nothing just happens. If you want things to happen, you have to make it happen. Whatever you plan to be or not be, you will be.

A plan is vital to the success that you see in life it's an essential key without it you will not see succeed

Every successful person planned to be where they currently are in their life. Where I am today in my life is because I planned it. I planned to become an author, otherwise you would not be reading this book. Every speech I have ever given I planned. Everything I have accomplished so far in my life I planned. Where you are now is where you planned to be whether it is something you are enjoying or not. A plan is like a roadmap, it shows you how to get to a specific destination. It creates a map for you on the road of life. If where you are now in life is not where you would like to be, then map out a different destination. A plan shows you where you are and where you are going. When using a navigation system to find a particular destination, that navigation first shows you where you are located, and then gives you directions to get to where you are going. On your way to your destination you will find multiple roads designed to get you to your destination. Some of those roads may be under construction and if you happen to travel one that is, you will be taking a detour. In life, you will have detours because nothing is ever perfect. Expect detours on the road to becoming. If you lose your job, you are just on a detour. If you cannot get the money to start a business, you are just on a detour. If you are filing bankruptcy, you are on a detour. If things keep getting in the way of your business plan, you are just on a detour. You must know that plans may change, the road to get to your destination may change, but the destination itself does not change. A plan is the navigation to life; it gives you directions to get to your destination, the future you. You cannot become the future you without a plan.

*Commit to the Lord whatever you do, and he will establish
your plans. The Lord works out everything to its proper
end— even the wicked for a day of disaster
Proverbs 16:3-4 NIV*

God wants you to commit and submit your plans to him so that he can make sure you succeed. He wants to become responsible for the success of your plans. When you allow God to become responsible for the success of your plans, then he will be accountable for all the provisions and resources needed to make your plans successful. What better person than God to hold liable for the success of your plans. God wants to be the one to work it out so that he gets the glory. Your success helps God keep a good reputation. He will work things out for you for his namesake. The better you look, the better he looks to those around you. For him to do anything in your life, you have to create a plan.

Are you submitting your plans to God so that he can make you a better version of yourself? Are you submitting your plans to him so that he can help you release the potential you have inside of you? Are you planning to set free the man or woman that is trapped inside of you? Are you planning to see what you are able to become? Life will always test your plans, that is why you have to plan how you are going to win before you pick the fight.

> *You are naive to think trouble won't come your way on your road to success.*

Every person I know who has made it in life, found trouble on their journey. You will find problems on your journey. When you have a plan to win despite the trouble that finds you, you will never be defeated. People without a plan will never win. You will find that in life, the ones without a plan will be poor because they do not plan for their profit. They do not plan to do anything productive; they plan nothing at all. There are thousands of people living on the streets as I write this book and most of them are great people, but where they are they planned to be. The people who never plan anything always think that things and situations will work out, but they do not work out. Instead, things work you out and once they work you out the result will not be anything you planned. Whatever you want to become, you have to plan to become. Success is simply waiting for a plan that it can bring into reality, a future that does not yet exist.

Webster defines a plan as a method worked out in advance for achieving some objective

A plan provides you with the ability to give meaning to time. Time will always exist as long as you live, but when a purpose is applied to time, time now has meaning. When you give meaning to time, it allows you to determine its use. Those who decide not to apply purpose to time are those who go with the flow of life and choose the way of poverty. Those who choose to become successful have 24 hours a day, and those who choose to remain in poverty have 24 hours a day. What is the major difference between the two? Time. The successful apply purpose to time, the poor just live in time.

The successful produce something in time while the poor produce nothing. Instead they live off of what the successful produce in time.

Those who want to become what they were born to be must apply purpose to time. The only way to impact your life and generation starts with giving meaning to time

Think about the successful people around you. How often do you see them waste time? That's because their time has purpose and meaning. Now think about the people around you who are unsuccessful. How often do they waste their time? Probably pretty often because their time has no meaning and no purpose attached. Successful people give meaning and purpose to unused time. What do you plan on doing with the next 24 hours? People who want to become more already know the answer to that question. Individuals who are not looking to become more are not concerned with such a question. Every day of my life I plan to do something that helps me become more. Whether that is reading a book, attending an event, studying my craft/gift or connecting with people that can help me become more. You will never become the person you see in the future without giving purpose to time. Whatever controls your time, controls your future. If a job controls your time it, controls your future. If television controls your time, it will control your future. If hanging out controls your time, it will control your future. If nothing controls your time, then nothing will be in your future. If a plan controls your time, then you will become exactly what you planned.

Without a plan, you will never be able to take charge of your future.

You will never see your vision, the future you become a reality without a plan. Inside you is something greater then you can imagine. The future is not outside of you, it is inside you. You are the inventor of your future. Everything I am today I predicted to become because I made plans to become it. Whatever you plan to be you will become. Whatever you don't plan to become, you will not be. If you plan to become nothing, well you probably can finish the sentence. Every successful person predicted their future because they invented it. Yes, you can predict the future with a plan.

Phil Knight predicted his future long before he started to live it.

Enrolled as a graduate student in the School of Business at Stanford University, he took a small business class. While attending class, the professor assigned a task where the students had to invent a new business. Knight mapped out a blueprint for a shoe company dealing specifically in sports. From this assignment, he wrote a paper called "Can Japanese Sports Shoes Do To German Sports Shoes What Japanese Cameras Did to German Cameras?" Writing that paper helped him discover the purpose for his life, to create a business dealing with athletic shoes. Graduating in 1962 with an MBA he decided not to waste

182

any time and went on a trip to Japan. While in Japan, he went to a manufacturing plant named Onitsuka. He discovered that the company created a tiger brand running shoe. Impressed by the quality of the shoe he secured a distribution deal with Onitsuka. Excited about his new venture, he returned home and immediately secured a job at an accounting firm to fund his business plan. Figuring that he might need a little more security, he formed a partnership with his former Coach Bill Bowerman, establishing Blue Ribbon Sports in 1964. The two eventually quit their jobs and went hard to work on their business; opening up a couple retails stores in Santa Monica, California, and Eugene, Oregon. The well thought out plan allowed Knight and Bowerman in the 1960's to enjoy the fruits of their labor. However, in the early 1970's a dispute broke out between Knight, Bowerman and their distributor, Onitsuka. That dispute pushed Knight and Bowerman to start the own manufacturing plant. During the startup of the new distribution center, an employee and good friend of Knight suggested naming the new company Nike after the Greek winged goddess of victory. That day Nike was Born. Knight planned from the very beginning to be the world's top designer in athletics products. Today Nike is considered the world's largest supplier and manufacture of athletic shoes and apparel. According to Forbes Nike's brand value is an estimated $15.9 billion.

Everything Knight became he planned to be; it wasn't by luck, it was by planning. Planning is a necessity of success, its vital to you becoming more and essential to you fulfilling your potential.

Planning impacts your life on so many levels

Planning helps you determine the use of your resources. Resources like your time, money, talent, energy, gifts, knowledge, house, and car. Planning determines the use of those resources. When you have a plan in place, you will not allow your resources to be abused. When you have a plan for your money, you will not allow it to be given away to people that won't help you fulfill your purpose. You won't waste your time playing taxi with people who cannot help you get to the next level. A plan won't let you spend hours upon hours talking with someone that can't help you succeed. A plan will not allow you to waste your energy on things that cannot help you become more. A plan will not allow you to continue to pour out your cup without someone filling you back up. If you are not being filled up every time you pour out of your cup, you are abusing your resources therefore, you need a plan not to. If you don't control your time, your things, your life, then other people will control your future.

The greatest act of faith and vision is a plan

I am a firm believer that if you believe in something, you execute. That which you do not believe in you, do not execute. For example, if I believe I can fly then I can climb to the top of a building and jump off, but since I do not believe that I can fly or that wings will pop out of my back, then I don't jump. Whatever you believe, you will do. Whatever you don't believe, you will not do. That's why a plan shows your belief in something, a plan compels you to execute what you believe. A plan is necessary to bring into reality what you believe. A plan in something that helps you to eliminate hope. I don't know if you have noticed this, but hopeful people are always broke because they continually hope. They hope things will happen instead of planning for things to happen. Have you ever been around a person that said I hope we own a house one day but they are still renting? I hope I get married someday, but they are still searching. I hope I become successful someday, but they are still sitting on the couch. I hope I can start a business one day, but they are still working for an employer. Please do not misunderstand me, hope is a great thing because it helps you to establish belief, but hope by itself is completely empty, so from today forward no more hoping and wishing, write down a plan.

A man's heart plans his way, But the Lord directs his steps. Proverbs 16:9

The word heart in this verse refers to the mind. Therefore, you are responsible for using your mind to make plans. God is not saying that you should wait for him to give you a plan. No, you sit down and give him a plan that comes from your mind. He wants you to write down a future on paper so that he can design the steps, timing, and processes necessary to get you where you plan to GO. If you don't have a future in mind then God has nothing to do. Give God something to do by making a plan.

It's time to turn your thoughts into reality

I once heard Jim Rohn say that it is ok to think but not to just be a thinker. It is ok to have a philosophy but not to just be a philosopher. It is okay to dream but not to just be a dreamer. You have to have a daily objective for your life, or you will be considered just a thinker, a dreamer, a hoper, or a wisher and those people never accomplish anything. Dreams don't change your life; hope doesn't change your life, wishing doesn't change your life, plans change your life. Make a commitment today to no longer be a thinker, a dreamer, a hoper, or wisher, but a planner, a doer, and an executor. Do not go to sleep tonight without creating an objective for the unused time that you will have tomorrow. You must learn to finish the day before you start it. When you wake up with an objective, you have finished the day before you ever start.

Your vision and dreams are real, but your plans will make them a reality. Your dreams want to become a reality in your life, but they cannot become a reality without first having a plan.

Chapter 11

A Designed Destination

The bottom line is: We must be working on arriving at the destination for which we were put on this planet -Yehuda Berg

I was entering a highway one day, and I heard the navigation say to me continue on this route for 15 miles and take exit 100 on the right. In route to my destination, I saw numerous of exits signs, and I thought why not get off at one of those exits instead of the exit I'm supposed to use. You are probably thinking because those exits will not take you to where you are trying to go. You are 100% correct, there are millions of people on Purpose Highway, but they don't know what exit leads them to their destination. When traveling down Purpose Highway, you will find many exits. Each exit is designed to take you somewhere. That somewhere will always be determined by the exit you choose. Every exit you decide to take is determined by a purpose. Every human being that exists in this world today was born to exit at a specific destination. You were born to arrive at a certain destination eventually. You may not know the exit to your destination at this moment, but your design will help you discover that destination.

Purpose is a Journey

Your destiny in life is something you will be able to identify as you climb higher on the mountain of life. You become more aware of your destination by taking the journey down Purpose Highway, the highway which God has uniquely designed for you.

You make known to me the path of life;
you will fill me with joy in your presence,
with eternal pleasures at your right hand.

- *Psalm 16:11 NIV*

Traveling down Purpose Highway will help you discover your God- given destiny. You can only discover it by taking the journey, by following your innate abilities, by investing and refining who you are. God made you the way you are for a reason, if you decide to be like someone else, you will not find the path God laid out for you. The path can only be discovered when you are being who God called you to be. You can only discover your destiny by operating in your work. We discuss in chapter 3 how your work is not your job, but what you are. When you began to travel down a road that was not designed for you, finding your destiny will be almost impossible. Many times, in life we take the wrong exits and those exits lead to destinations that we should have never arrived at. Take a look at your current destination. Have you arrived at a place in life that is not you? If your answer to this question is yes, then you have left the Purpose Highway and got off at the wrong exit. Many times, the exits that pull us off Purpose Highway are distractions. Distractions are screaming exit signs that lead you in a wrong direction.

Travel the road of your GIFT

You will not find your destination traveling a different road then the one of your design. Many people don't discover their destination because they take exits that were not designed for them. You will always discover your destination when you are traveling on the road of your gift. Your purpose will only be found traveling the road of function and design. When you travel down the road of function and design, it will lead you to Purpose Highway. You read in chapter two and three that your functions and designs make up who you are, if you do not to travel down the road of what makes you who you are, then how can you find Purpose Highway. If I was designed to act and all of the functions that God gave me are acting abilities but instead I choose to become an accountant, then my life will always feel void and meaningless. I'm doing something I was never designed to do even though I may be good at it.

You will never find your purpose doing something that does not fit your design.

I had a few friends who loved to go 4-wheeling. One day we all went out 4-wheeling and another mutual friend of ours came along who had just bought a 2-wheel drive Jeep. We had fun for hours on this incredible dirt trail that one of my friends found. My friend with the 2-wheel drive jeep was doing surprisingly well, but the dirt began to get a little muddy. Eventually, he got stuck and could not get out because the car did not have a 4-wheel drive function like the other vehicles. A 2-wheel drive vehicle was never designed to go 4- wheeling on muddy dirt roads because it lacked the functions necessary to get the job done. Many people look for jobs and take careers that they were never designed for. They do things and take part in things that don't fit their design. Time after time we try to fit a square in a circle and it never fits. I'm a speaker and for me to try to travel down a path as a singer would be for me to commit Purpose Suicide.

Do things that will allow you to be yourself

When you do something God never designed you to do, you are not yourself and when you are not being yourself, life is no longer enjoyable, it is a complete struggle. The feeling of doing something you were designed for fulfills your heart's desire; locating your life's purpose. There is no greater feeling than doing something that allows you to be you. When you are doing something that permits you to be you, people have to tell you to stop working because you never get tired of being yourself. That is why it is essential to follow your design.

Your design leads you down the road to becoming yourself. Doing things you were not designed to do causes you to travel down the wrong road. Traveling the wrong road leads you to a false destination. When you travel to a destination God never designed for you, it forces you to separate yourself from your true nature. You will never become you, you will be something you were not designed to be. Acting outside of who you are will design a person that you will become disappointed in. I have found that people who complain the most about their jobs and their lives are those who are living a life that is not a part of their design. Sometimes we get confused because we become good at something and we think that it must be a fit because "I'm good at it". If you do something enough, eventually you become good at it. Would you do what you are doing without getting paid or recognized? Would you do it as a hobby? Would you do it to the point that people have to tell you to stop? Does it fill the purpose void in your life? Does it continuously fell like work? If you could stop it and do something else, would you? If you answered honestly to most of those questions, then what you are good at is not what you were designed to do. If you were designed to do it, then the answers to those questions will either confirm that you are operating within your design or you are allowing life to mold you into something you are not.

Follow your design

When you do something that connects you to your design, you will find fulfillment, happiness, and opportunities. To follow your design is to follow your gift and when you follow your gift, it will lead you to Purpose Highway and Purpose Highway will take you to your destination, your (life's purpose). I compel you, start traveling down the road of your design so that it helps you locate Purpose Highway. If you were designed to teach, then travel that road. If you were designed to game, then travel that road. If you were designed to make music, then travel that road. Don't take a job that takes you down a different road. Find a job that takes you toward the road you were designed to travel until you are able to make a living from your work. If you were designed to teach, do not take a job as an accountant, find a job that will allow you to use the functions you were born with.

You must not allow people to trap your design.

People will try to place you in a box and the moment you realize that, your design will not allow you to fit in that box, you will be judge and criticized. God did not design everyone to be a part of the five-fold ministry. Everyone was not designed to be an Apostle, Prophet, Evangelist, Pastor or Teacher. If you decide to follow something that is not a part of your design, then you will never find the destination that God ordained for you.

Your destination is in your design, not the design that other people want you to be. You are the way you are because God planned for you to be that way, so follow your design. People are going to criticize and judge you when you don't conform to their idea of what and who you should be. If God designed you to travel a certain road, then travel it no matter what people think. They criticized Jesus because he did not look like them nor could they place him in a box Follow your design and God will bless you on the path he called you to travel.

I must warn you, when you enter Purpose Highway things get a little tough because life has a unique way of testing you. Traveling down Purpose Highway will cause many distractions along the way. If you have ever traveled a highway, you will notice that there are exits about every mile. Each exit leads to a different road. The only reason you don't exit every time is because it does not take you to your destination. The way you were designed and how you were made to function are inseparable to your purpose in life. If you were designed to sing, then music is a part of your purpose and you cannot separate the two. If you are designed to inspire people, then being a leader will become a part of your purpose you cannot separate the two. Your design helps you fulfill your purpose. The way you function and how you are designed are the key components to fulfilling your purpose. Your purpose will never be outside of your functions and design. Your functions determine the way you were designed so that you can fulfill your purpose. That's why you just can't take any exit on Purpose Highway, it has to be the exit that fits your functions and design.

Distractions kill dreams, visions, and plans

There are no wrong or bad exits on a highway. If you happen to take a wrong exit, it won't be because you thought it was wrong or bad, but because you thought it was okay. This is how distractions find their way into your life.

Distractions will never appear to be wrong or bad. Distractions appear to be good, otherwise how could they distract you? I find this to be the number one purpose killer. I have watched distractions kill dreams, visions, and purpose.

When traveling down Purpose Highway, so many things will try to get you to exit. Many leave Purpose Highway to travel down a road that will inevitably lead them to a destination that does not align with their functions or a design which will eventually lead them to an unhappy and unfulfilling life. People will try to pull you away and it will be the ones you think are not a distraction. Anything that pulls you away from operating in your function and design is a distraction. Money can become a distraction.

A job can pay you more in an effort to keep you operating in something that you were not designed to do. Problems can become a distraction because they can take your focus away from doing what you were designed to do. Opportunities can become distractions because they offer benefits that cause you to abort your function and design. What is distracting you from operating in your gift? Is it people? Is it money? Is it an opportunity? Is it a problem?

What is it? You will never reach your destination being distracted by exits that have nothing to do with your gift. Your gift is the only thing that can lead you to your purpose, nothing else can.

On your way to your destination, trouble is going to come at you, but you must keep going until you arrive at the place you were designed for

I was listening to the testimony of T.D Jakes. At 26 years old, Bishop Jakes explained how he hit a pothole in life. He lost his job and his income. Devastated by the loss of his job, he feared he was not going to be able to feed his family. He said that this put him in a state of depression. He explained how he had no car and had to take community transportation because his car was repossessed by the bank. No way to pay his electric bill, they shut off his power. Somehow with the ability to still go on, he went to his neighbor's house to use their phone to look for job opportunities. Life had knocked Bishop Jakes down but he kept going because he had a destination that he said he had to reach.

Life comes at you hard, but you must not stop going after your destination. Trouble does not last. Things do change and new days do come, but your destination has to remain a constant pursuit. Since Bishop Jakes' destination remained clear, despite every obstacle that he faced, he was able to persevere. He is one of the world's most influential preachers, speakers and business leaders today because he never stopped pursuing his destination. You have to maintain your focus on the destination because it will lead you to your success. Success is waiting for you. The road is never easy, but as long as you continue to travel down Purpose Highway, I promise it will lead you to an exit. That exit will cause you to use your gift/s to contribute to your generation, and this is your destiny, this is your purpose, this is where you find your success.

Chapter 12

Your Designed Contribution

When you cease to make a contribution, you begin
to die.
-Eleanor Roosevelt

Your contribution to your generation ultimately becomes your purpose. It becomes the meaning of your existence. The way you were made to function and designed are what equip you with all the abilities you will ever need to fulfill your contribution to your generation. You were born to make a contribution, that's why you feel void and purposelessness when you are not contributing to your generation. That void compels you to ask yourself questions like, why am I here? What was I created for? What is my purpose? Does my life have meaning? Your purpose is your unique contribution to the world. All the abilities that you have inside of you were given to you to serve. It is in serving those abilities that you find your purpose. The fulfillment in life that you long for begins with serving others. There is no true fulfillment in serving yourself. Your fulfillment comes in serving others your gift. Material things and self-service will never bring you true happiness because they are temporary. The pleasure of getting something new wears off quickly. You can collect all the material things you want in life and you will find that when the storms of life come your way, the stuff you have collected does not matter. It cannot truly help you or others. Accumulating stuff will never bring you the joy that helping someone else will. When you begin serving your gift, it will give you a high like no high other on this earth. I can tell you this from my own personal experience, there is no greater feeling than knowing that you helped someone out of their pit.

The meaning to your life will be found in serving your gift/s

God did not give you innate abilities just to make your life better. You were born with them because they are to be shared. The day you discover your gift and serve it to the world is the day you discover your purpose. It is the day you find meaning; it is the day you find your why for existing. Your meaning is inherited in the gift/s God gave you and your purpose is to serve that gift/s. The world is waiting for you. Just imagine if Steve Jobs did not share his gift with us. There would be no iPad or iPhone. What if Elon Musk did not share his gift for improving the world? There would be no Tesla or Space X. What if Phil knight never shared his gift for quality athletic shoes? There would be no Nike. Everything that you will use today comes from someone deciding to share their gift. What gifts are you refusing to share that someone can benefit from? What abilities are you hiding that the world could use? The success you seek is waiting for you, but it will only be found in serving your gift.

Monica Yunus

When operating in your gift, it will bring you to levels you never thought possible, but those levels are not to be a service to you, but to the generation you were born to serve. This was the case for Monica Yunus. Born in Bangladesh, Yunus and her mother found her way to the United States when Yunus was four months old after her mother and father ended their marriage. Yunus's mother decided that Bangladesh was not a place to raise a child, so she took Yunus to New Jersey and moved in with her parents. At a very young age, Yunus's grandmother noticed that she had a gifted voice. Yunus's grandmother became very influential in helping her develop her gift by putting her in a church choir. Doing this, Yunus's grandmother helped her become aware of her gift and of her love for music. Though-out Yunus's childhood, her mother and grandmother helped her hone in on her gift leading her to become a well-known name in the opera world by the age of 15. She continued to develop her gift by enrolling in Juilliard and majoring in Vocal Performance. After graduating, Yunus secured spots in several professional operas. Her career in music became a success. While operating in the success of her gift, she looked for a way to contribute to her generation. In 2004, she got that opportunity. She co-founded and is currently the director of Sing For Hope — a nonprofit organization based in New York that brings arts programming to underprivileged communities. Yunus is now using her gift to make a difference. Her gift bought her success and influence. She uses that success and influence to contribute to her generation.

Selfish people don't like sharing

Your gift is a service that you were born with. That service was given to you to share. It is in sharing your gift that creates a new world for you. What do you have to share? Selfish people can never truly understand purpose because their only desire is self- assurance. They care about no one but themselves and that is why they will never be fulfilled. They will always feel a void in their life. They will never find meaning because all they care about is their success and well- being. Zig Ziegler said, "if you help enough people get what they want, you will always have what you want." Notice also that if you help others get what they want, you will always find the success you seek.

I was reading the Huffington Post one day and came across a compelling story of the sharing of gifts. The story was shared by Arianna Huffington in her book, Thrive. It was a story about her sister, Agappi, who graduated from the Royal Academy of Dramatic Art in London. Despite the success she saw and the awards she received, she was hit with a devastating blow when she didn't get a part she auditioned for in a theatre play. This caused her to second guess her gift. Leaving the audition discouraged, she met a stranger on the public city bus and they begin to converse about theatre plays randomly. This caused Agappi to open up about the experience she just had. One thing led to another and Agappi started to do a short monologue for the woman she had just met. That monologue affected the women in a way that caused her to break out in tears because she was so moved by the acting of Agappi. At this moment Agappi no longer felt discouraged but encouraged by her gift to perform. It was on that bus that she learned a valuable lesson: In her words, "That moment of sharing without an agenda of getting a part wasn't about the outcome, but about the joy of touching others and giving unconditionally what was mine to give. And that brought with it a tremendous sense of fulfillment."

You never work being yourself

If you honestly pay attention to the successful people around you, you will find that they have one thing in common, they provide a service to others. Serving your gift is the thing that will bring you opportunities far beyond your imagination. Serving your gift is responsible for the success you see in life. People who discover and serve their innate abilities are more efficient in their performance and live a higher quality of life. Serving your natural abilities gives you the opportunity to remain yourself. Being yourself causes you to stress less, increases your positive emotions, and adds more get-up-and-go to your day because there is no greater feeling than being yourself. You never work serving yourself to others.

Serving Your gift will open doors

Serving your gift will cause people with influence to find you. Serving your gift makes you valuable. The gift/s you were born to serve will attract money. Your gift, with proper development and use will create for you richness beyond your imagination, in all aspects of your life. When you serve the gift/s, you were born with, doors and windows will begin to open far and wide for you. Whatever you put into your gift is what life will give back to you. Your gift is waiting to provide you with a remarkable life. Your gift is an investment. If you don't capitalize on it, it will never grow. You will lose the compounding interest you and others can benefit from.

Never change the path your gift creates for you

There was a gentleman by the name of Paul Terasaki's. Paul life did not start out promising for him. He was born to Japanese immigrants during World War 2. During the war, he and his family were forced into the internment program that relocated people of his decent to camps and deprived them of living the American dream.

Living in Chicago until he graduated high school, allowed enough time to past, so he and his family were able to move back to California after the war. This is where Terasaki enrolled at UCLA to study Zoology. While earning

213

his Master's degree, he wrote a thesis that familiarized him with transplantation science. It was the discovery of transplantation science that ignited his gift. While completing his postdoctoral degree at the UK college in London, he was working for the predecessor of transplantation biology, Sir Peter Medawar. Working with Medawar stirred Terasaki's gift for science. After spending one year in London, Teraski returned to UCLA in 1956 and joined the department of surgery as an assistant research zoologist. This led him to a deep interest in cellular and molecular basis of tissue rejection. This interest steered Terasaki into creating and developing what became known as the Micro-cytotoxicity assay. This allows doctors and the like to determine blood types quickly or what he would call, HLA types for both a recipient and donor. This coincided with the first stirrings of what was to be the discovery of the HLA system. HLA typing had already existed in those days, but the techniques used were very unreliable and tedious. So, a Professor from oxford's Weatherall Institute of Molecular Medicine was working at Stanford University in California where he discovered Terasaki's micro-cytotoxicity assay in the mid to late 1960's. After this, the test soon became the international standard test because it only required small amounts of material. Terasaki, who had no qualifications in medicine, created a registry that collected all of the data on all of the transplants which eventually led to the system we have today of organ sharing priorities and the like.

Terasaki Testing system was born out of his gift, and that gift made him a very wealthy man. Using the proceeds from his gift, he began creating the Terasaki Family foundation supporting the Terasaski Research Institute that is devoted to cancer immunotherapy and the study of immunity and transplantation. It was Terasaki's gift that saved many lives in the 1970's because he discovered his gift and shared it with the world. The discovery of his gift allowed people to find like-organ donors promptly so that their life could be saved from a transplant. Terasaki was never looking for money, as a matter of fact, they had to force him to start a business because all he wanted to do was serve his gift. Wealth found him when he began serving his gift to the world.

The pleasure is in serving

When I discovered my gift, I realized to serve would be to teach others how to identify their gift/s. My gift is to help people find their gift/s, otherwise there would be no reason for the creation of this book. This book you are reading is me sharing my gift with you. I did not write this book for money (even though money shows up in the process). I wrote this book to help you discover the unique gift/s you were given. Nothing brings me more pleasure than knowing that this book will help transform lives. When you get me, you get a teacher and a speaker who was designed to help others find their gift and discover themselves.

My passion lies in helping people discover their true self, who they are designed to become. Nothing makes me angrier than seeing someone waste their gift/s. It twists me in such a way that I can't explain. That is because I am passionate about people's gift/s, that is the gift that has been given to me. I have invested in the lives of so many people's gift/s that it has crippled my family at times. My wife had to put the brakes on me because I love to see people operating in their gift and I would invest all the money we had into them not knowing that people would take advantage of these resources. Those experiences taught me a lot about myself. It helps me recognize people who want to discover themselves and the ones who don't. Now I can recognize where to invest my resources and that's in people like you, or you would not be reading this book. I offer you a gift, a 30-minute consulting session. If you are unsure or have questions concerning your gift, please give our office a call or visit us at www.designedtobecomemore.com because I want nothing more than for you to become who you were designed to be. My life assignment and purpose is to help you discover the gift you were born with and I will do whatever is in my power to do so. What purpose do you serve in the lives of others? When you go away, what goes with you?

You were born to solve a problem. I was born to help others discover what is inside of them. I am a gift influencer. I influence people to find who they were designed to become. I was designed to help you answer the question, "what am I gifted at? I was born to bring things that are hidden inside you to light so that you can discover who you are. I am the response to people not knowing their gift/s. I am the response to untapped potential. I am the response to self- discovery. What problem were you born to respond to? Joe Gebbia was designed to solve the problem of unaffordable lodging during travel or everyday living. He has made it possible for 260 million people in 65,000 cities to find affordable lodging. Joe Gebbia is the Co-Founder of Airbnb, a person to person home and apartment rental company. His services created a net worth of $3.3 billion for him according to Forbes. Jack Ma was designed to solve the problem of small business exportation. Small businesses in China had no way of selling and exporting products they produced to other markets, so Jack Ma created Alibaba to solve that problem. So now, many small businesses in China have become very successful today thanks to Jack Ma. This contribution to his country has made him worth $40.3 billion according to Forbes. Jesus came to earth to reestablish our connection with God. He solved the problem that sin created which was separation from God. We now can go directly to God because of the contribution Jesus made to humanity.

When you discover your gift/s and begin serving it, you will find that it deploys you. It is in serving your gift/s that you will find your business. There is a reason you were born where you were, to the parents you were born to and even the journey that you have been through thus far. You were prepared for this particular generation that you have been assigned to, what will you contribute to it?

Your Gift makes you Influential

Every person on this planet was born with a seed. A gift that is uniquely his or hers. Your gift is like your DNA. No one has the same DNA although everyone has DNA. Your gift is uniquely designed, no one else has it. Your gift is your natural resource, you have to dig to discover it and once you do, you have to remove the dust and polish your gifts so that you can use it to become an influence to your generation. Your gift gives you the power to influence others in a way that will affect action and change within them. It gives you the ability to capture the hearts and minds of people. Your gift is designed to make you influential when you discover and serve it. We have established that your gift is not for you but for others. You were born with influence.

Your gift is that influence. Influence is discovering your gift and its contribution. When you find who you were designed to serve, you find your influence. I'm designed to help people discover their unique gift and design. Therefore, my influence is helping people discover their gift/s and who they are designed to become. Who are you designed to serve? Nelson Mandela and Martin Luther King Jr. were designed to serve those who suffered injustice. Walt Disney was designed to serve kids by creating a world of entertainment specially designed for kids. Sam Walton was designed to serve local communities by creating jobs and saving people money by selling more for less. Wright brothers were designed to serve in global transportation by helping people get places faster in a shorter amount of time. Clara Barton was designed to serve those in need during disasters and catastrophic times. She is the founder of the American Red Cross, a humanitarian organization that provides emergency assistance, disaster relief and education in the United States.

Bill Gates and Steve Jobs were designed to serve in the advancement of technology by creating technology that everyday people could use to advance their own lives. Sara Blakely was designed to serve the body of women. She created a product called Spanx that helped shape the trouble areas of women's bodies giving them a flawless figure.

If you follow the lives of every individual I just named, you will notice that their influence came from of their gift. Influence was not given to them by the things they create, the education they received or by their fame. Their influence came only because of their willingness to find a way to serve their unique gift to mankind. None of these men or women sought to become influential, they were focused on refining and serving their unique gift and they became influential by being themselves. You do not need to become anyone else but yourself to make an impact on the world. You just have to discover what you were designed to be and allow that design to be a service to your generation. You will know when you are serving your design in the area you are gifted in when people start looking for you in that area.

My wife has a gift for fashion and beauty. When people want something done or have a question concerning fashion or beauty they find her because it is a part of her design. The influence that she holds are in those areas. When you serve your gift in the area you were designed to serve, you will discover your significance to your generation and that significance brings influence, and that influence comes from the value of your gift. That's why this book was created, everyone on earth has an inherent design to become something great. Who and what they are is an individual discovery and I hope reading this book has brought you a step closer to the discovering yourself.

Once you find and refine your gift, it will create a life that you have not imagined. Make a promise to yourself that you'll dig to find your natural resource, so that the world may benefit. Make it a personal mandate to discover your design.

NOTES

Chapter 1
Wikipedia definition page 11
Vera wang Business of Fashion Website page 12
Webster definition page 14
Google searches page 16
Thomas Nelson, Tyndale House Foundation, Biblica Inc
NKJV NLT NIV pages 21-34

Chapter 2
Biblica Inc NIV page 53
Webster definition page 35 Biblica Inc page 54
Finding your Element by Ken Robinson page 60

Chapter 3
Tyndale House Foundation page 64
Biblica Inc page 65-66
Stanford New webstie
https://news.stanford.edu/2005/06/14/jobs- 061505/ page
68
Pursuit of Purpose by Myles Munroe page 74

Chapter 4
Biblica Inc page 80

Chapter 5
Thomas Nelson page 92,97
Biblica inc page 93
Tyndale House Foundation page 101

Chapter 6
Thomas Nelson page 106
Dr. Myles Munroe page 107
Kevin Plank Under Armour website
http://www.uabiz.com/company/history.cfm page 115

Chapter 7
Bible verse by Biblica inc page 118
Psychologists Ulrich Weger and Stephen Loughnan
https://www.scientificamerican.com/article/your-thoughts-
can- release-abilities-beyond-normal-limits/ page 127
Bible verse by Thomas Nelson page 132

Chapter 8
Bible verse Thomas Nelson page 137
Lindsey Vonn Mindbodygreen website
www.mindbodygreen.com page 141
Arnold Schwarzenegger Mindbodygreen website
www.mindbodygreen.com page 144
Bible verse Thomas Nelson page 145

Chapter 9
Mother Teresa https://www.biography.com/people/mother-
teresa-9504160 page 155
Wendy Kopp http://www.achievement.org/achiever/wendy-
kopp/ Page 158
National Public radio interview page 159
J.K Rowling https://www.biography.com/people/jk-
rowling-40998 page 162
Bible verse Tyndale House Foundation page 169

Chapter 10
Warren Buffett https://www.biography.com/people/warren-buffett- 9230729 page 172
Bible verse by Biblica inc page 177
Phil Knight https://www.entrepreneur.com/article/197534 page 182
Bible verse by Biblica inc page 187

Chapter 11
Bible verse by Biblica Inc page 191

Chapter 12
Monica Yunus
https://en.wikipedia.org/wiki/Monica_Yunus page 208
Huffington Post Arianna Huffington Thrive page 210
Paul Terasaki's http://www.onelambda.com/en/about-us/news/recent-news/terasaki-news.html page 213
Joe Gebbia Airbnb https://www.forbes.com/profile/joe-gebbia/ page 219

For a free 30-minute gift consultation please visit
www.designedtobecomemore.com
or email us at findmygift@designedtobecomemore.com

84199203R00138

Made in the USA
Lexington, KY
20 March 2018